CONTENTS

MICROORGANISMS	06
WHAT ARE PARASITES?	08
COMMON PARASITES	10
GOOD AND BAD BACTERIA	12
BACTERIAL HABITATS	14
BACTERIAL DISEASES	16
PROTOZOA	18
PROTOZOAN DISEASES	20
HELMINTHS	22
HELMINTHIC DISEASES	24
FUNGI	26
FUNGAL DISEASES	28
PARASITIC VECTORS	30
COMMON MODES OF PARASITE TRANSMISSION	32
STUDY OF INFECTIOUS DISEASES	34
EPIDEMICS AND PANDEMICS IN HISTORY	36
STERILISATION AND DISINFECTION	38
ANTIBIOTICS	40
VACCINATION	42
BEST PRACTICES	44
INTRODUCTION TO CORONAVIRUS	46
A BRIEF OVERVIEW OF PANDEMICS	48
FROM ORIGIN TO TRANSMISSION	50
CORONAVIRUS OUTBREAK	52
OUTLOOK AND AFTERMATH	54
SAFETY AND PREVENTIVE MEASURES	56
THE STEALTHY VIRUS AND REMEDIES	58
GLOBAL IMPACT	60

MICROORGANISMS

The term 'microorganism' (or 'microbe') applies to a wide range of microscopic organisms such as bacteria, fungi, protozoa, and algae. Viruses are microscopic too; however, they are not considered to be true living organisms. There are several known and unknown microbe species, many that are free-living and others that depend on other living organisms or hosts.

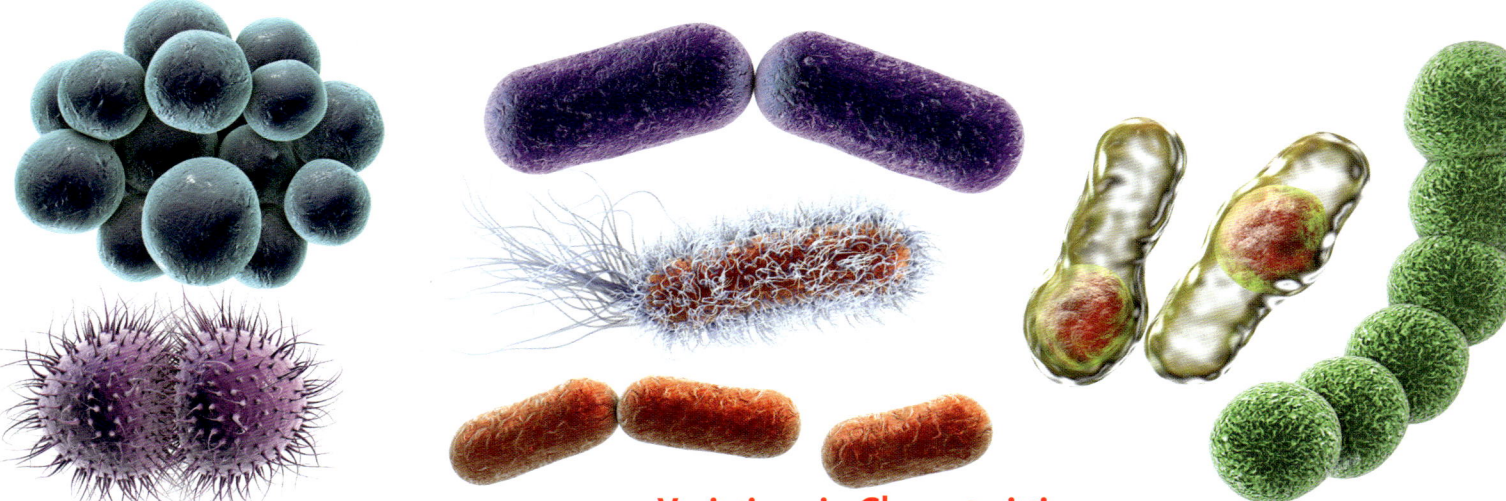

❋ Microbes come with a variety of shapes, sizes, and features

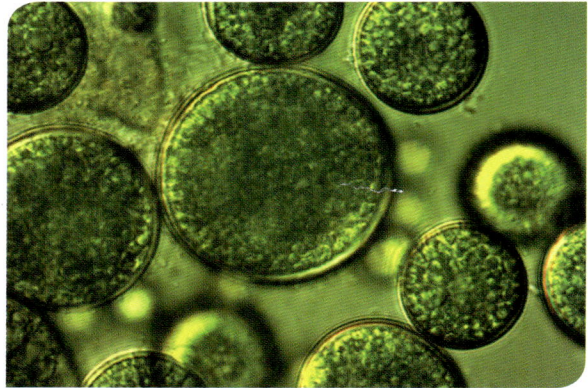

❋ Green algae, like plants, can manufacture their own food from water and sunlight

Variations in Characteristics

Microbes vary in size from less than 100 nanometres (1 nanometre is one-billionth of a metre) to about 1 millimetre (visible to the eye). All unicellular organisms under Archaea and Bacteria are classified as microbes. All the organisms under these domains are prokaryotes. Eukaryotes include multicellular organisms as well as unicellular organisms under protists and protozoa. Interestingly, the protists resemble plants or animals and include many unique microbes.

Many multicellular species of fungi and algae are microscopic and not visible to the eye. Microbes have adapted to survive in almost all of earth's habitats including the poles, deserts, rocks, air – even in extreme environments such as hydrothermal vents, geysers, and the deep sea.

Algae: Among microorganisms, the green algae are photosynthetic and capable of producing their own food, much like plants, and are hence known as autotrophs. Some algae are classified under protists while others resemble terrestrial plants.

Bacteria: All bacterial species are prokaryotic and unicellular. Bacterial cells do not have well-defined nuclei and each individual cell reproduces to produce two daughter cells. Many species aggregate to form colonies or clumps.

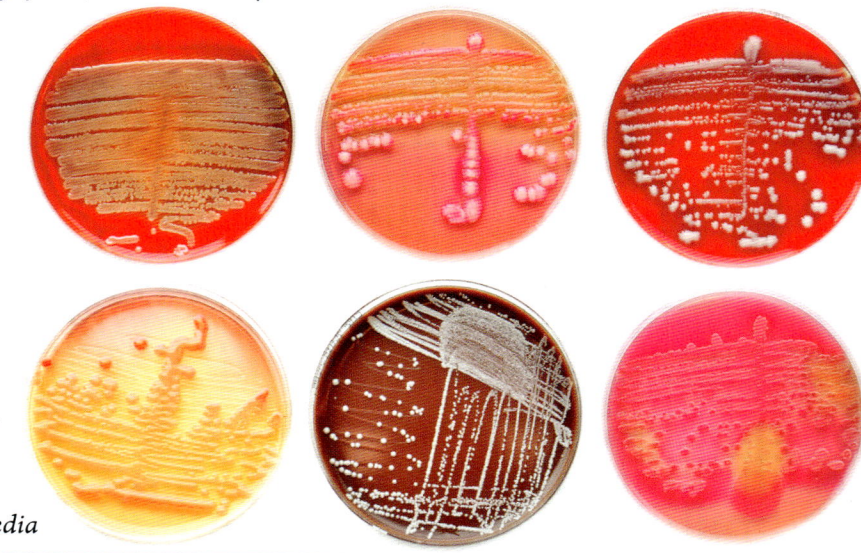

❋ Bacterial colony grown in special media

Fungi: Fungi include microscopic as well as macroscopic species. Mushroom and mould spores are visible to the eye whereas unicellular species such as baker's yeast or fission yeast are not. Fungi exhibit immense diversity in characteristic features. One fungal species, Candida albicans, is capable of switching between growing as single cells and filamentous hyphae depending on the environment.

❋ *Candida cells can develop hyphae when needed*

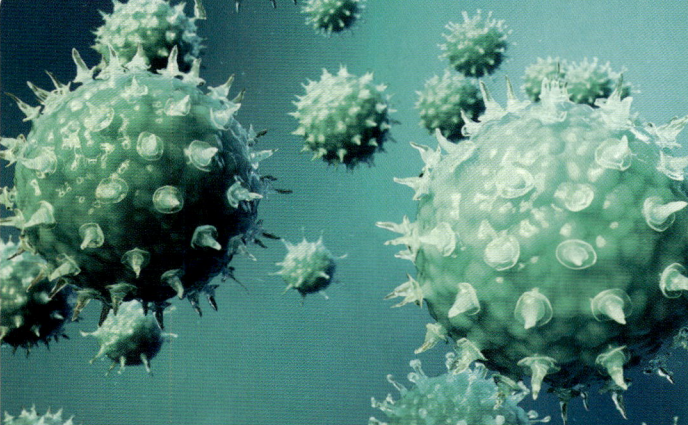

❋ *Viruses are not considered strictly as "living parasites"*

Protists: Among eukaryotes, protists are microscopic and unicellular and include a diverse range of organisms that are often difficult to classify under one group.

Protozoa: They are unicellular eukaryotic organisms that are free-living or existing as parasites inside hosts. They exhibit "animal-like" characteristics including motility and predation and do not possess cell walls.

Viruses: Viruses are obligate intracellular parasites that do not exhibit any signs of life outside the host. They have only limited biological function and different viruses are capable of infecting organisms ranging from bacteria to humans.

❋ *Microbes found normally on skin surface*

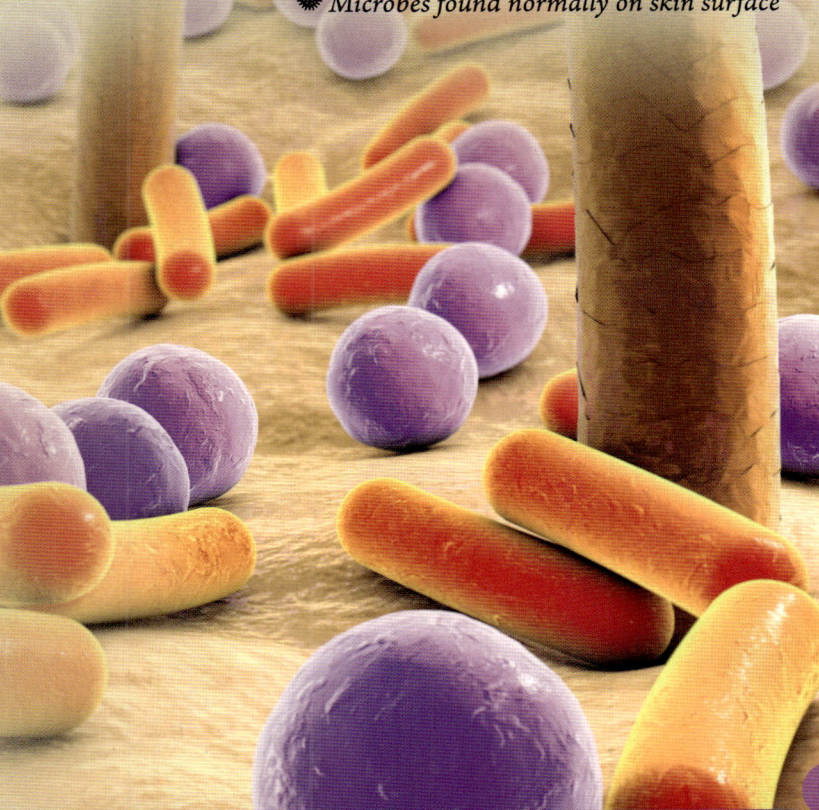

Fact File
Thiomargarita namibiensis at 750 micrometres (or 0.75 millimetre) in size is the largest known bacterium ever discovered.

Microbes and Humans

Microbes have played an important role in human culture ranging from being used for fermenting foods for thousands of years to sewage treatment, fuel production, and synthesis of enzymes and bioactive compounds in recent years. Many microbes, including several bacterial species, are part of the regular microbiota that live in the gut and skin.

WHAT ARE PARASITES?

Different organisms interact with each other in different ways. Parasitism is a relationship in which one organism benefits while causing harm to the other organism, often referred to as host. Parasites are almost always much smaller than their hosts and get their nutrients directly from their host, usually at its expense, and live within the host for an extended period of time.

What Parasites Do

Parasitism is similar to "predation" in which one organism feeds on another. However, there is one major difference between a predator and a parasite. A predator is often bigger than the prey and kills the prey to feed on it. A parasite is many thousand times smaller than the host and enters into the body to feed on the host's nutrients. A parasite also does not immediately kill the host, sometimes residing for several months to years within the host.

Parasites that target animals are highly specialized and capable of reproducing at a much faster pace than the host itself. Among parasites that affect humans, the ones capable of causing disease include:

- Protozoa
- Heminths
- Ectoparasites

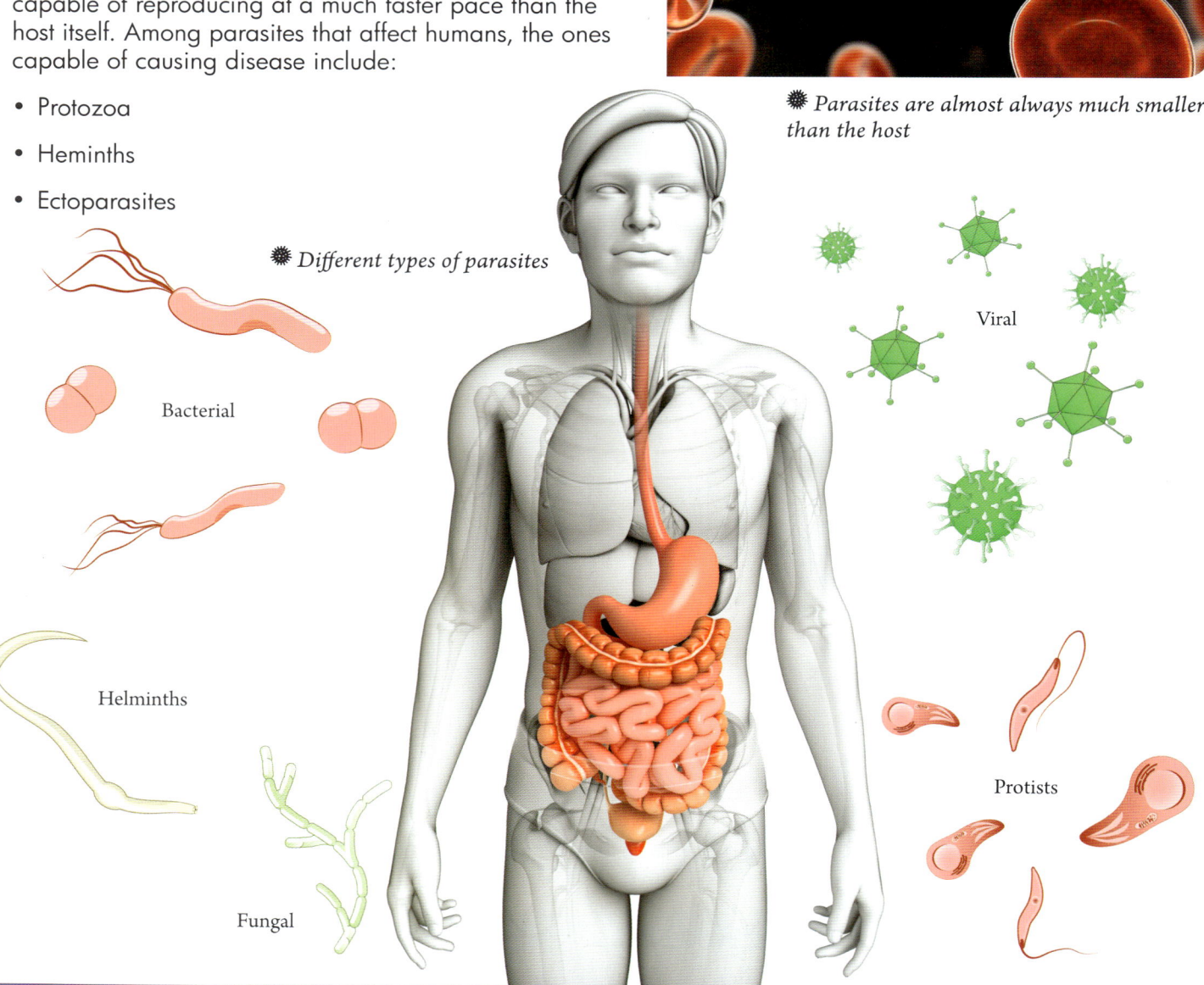

❋ *Parasites are almost always much smaller than the host*

❋ *Different types of parasites*

Bacterial

Viral

Helminths

Fungal

Protists

Classifying Parasites

Biologists have classified parasites based on different criteria and based on their mode of survival they are classified as ectoparasites or endoparasites. Ectoparasites lives on the outer surface of a host while feeding on its nutrients while endoparasites live inside the host. Head lice and ticks are examples of ectoparasites that live in hair or fur and feed on blood. Tapeworms and bacteria live inside the host and absorb nutrients from the host.

An obligate parasite is completely dependent on the host for survival while a facultative parasite is not. Chlamydia is a bacterial species that grows only within a living host. Armillaria is a fungal parasite that infects trees but even after the tree dies, it continues to eat the dead wood.

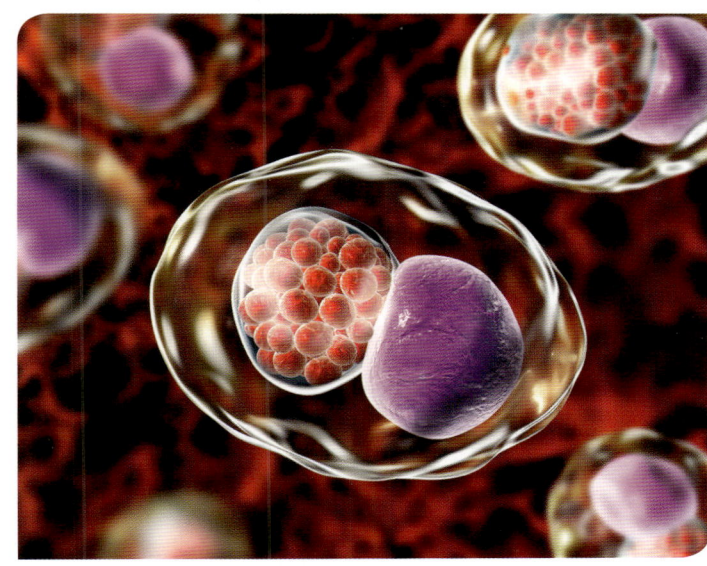

✤ *Chlamydia bacteria can only grow in live hosts*

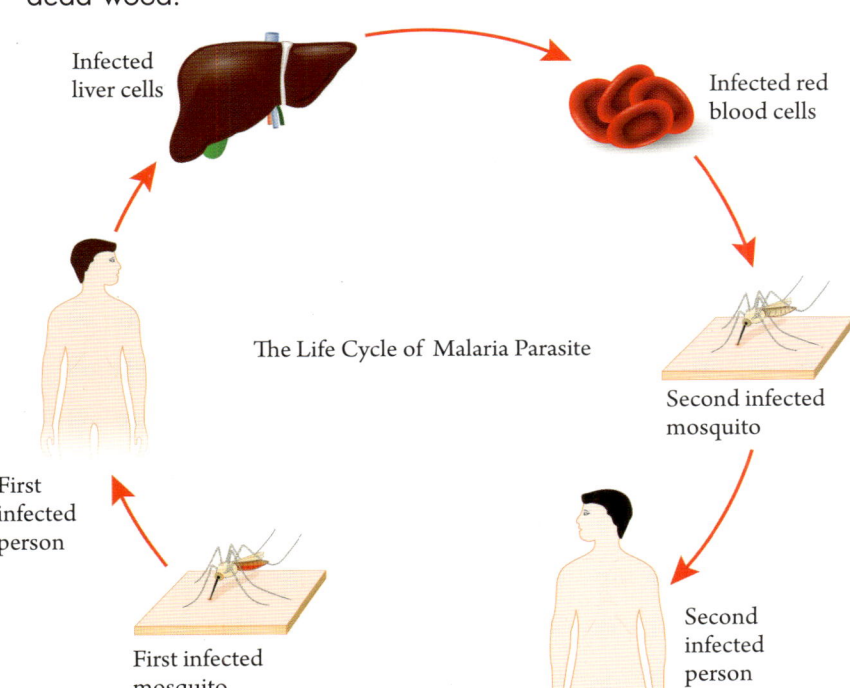

✤ *Malarial parasites have a life cycle involving both mosquitoes and humans*

Microparasites are those microbes such as bacteria and viruses that are capable of completing their life cycles inside the host while macroparasites reproduce and complete their life cycle outside the host. Parasites either have direct life cycles, which involve only one host, or indirect life cycles, which involve one main and one other intermediate host.

Parasites and Hosts

Parasites increase their fitness and growth while reducing the host fitness and causing modifications in host behavior. Parasites identify a potential host using sensory cues such as vibration, carbon dioxide, skin odor, moisture, and visual and heat signatures.

Fact File
"Parasite" is derived from a Greek word "parasitos" which means "someone who eats at the table of another"!

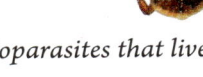

✤ *Bed bugs are ectoparasites that live outside the skin*

COMMON PARASITES

Several species of bacteria, viruses, and fungi cause diseases in humans, plants, and other animals. Ectoparasites such as lice, ticks, and bed bugs attach to the skin and feed on blood. Apart from ectoparasites, the other major classes of parasites include protozoa and helminths.

Protozoa

Protozoa are unicellular microscopic organisms that are either free-living or parasitic in nature. Among the parasites, certain protozoan species multiply in suitable hosts such as humans. Protozoa that reside in the intestine occur through the fecal or oral route. Those that live in the blood or tissues are transmitted through the bites of mosquitoes or sand flies.

Protozoa that infect humans are classified into four types:

- Sarcodina (Amoeba)
- Mastigophora (Leishmania, Giardia)
- Ciliophora (Balantidium)
- Sporozoa (Plasmodium)

❋ *Protozoa with hair-like cilia all over the surface*

Helminths

Helminths are large, multicellular organisms that are visible when they mature into adults. Helminths are either free-living or parasitic. Helminths cannot multiply inside humans once they turn into adults.

The three main types of helminths include:

- Flatworms (Flukes and Tapeworms)
- Thorny-headed worms
- Roundworms (Nematodes)

※ *Helminth worms are large enough to be visible and multiply inside human hosts*

Ectoparasites

Blood-sucking insects such as mosquitoes, ticks, fleas, lice, mites, and flies are dependent on humans for survival. Some attach to the skin and remain with the host for weeks or months. Even though the ectoparasites are capable of causing diseases on their own, they also act as vectors that transmit pathogenic microbes from one host to another.

Parasitic infections are a huge burden on regions with tropical and subtropical climates and also temperate climates. Malaria, in particular, is a leading cause of death every year across the world.

Fact File
Euglena, which are capable of movement as well as photosynthesis, are classified as both protozoa and algae!

※ *Ectoparasites, such as this cat flea, live outside the host and usually suck blood for survival*

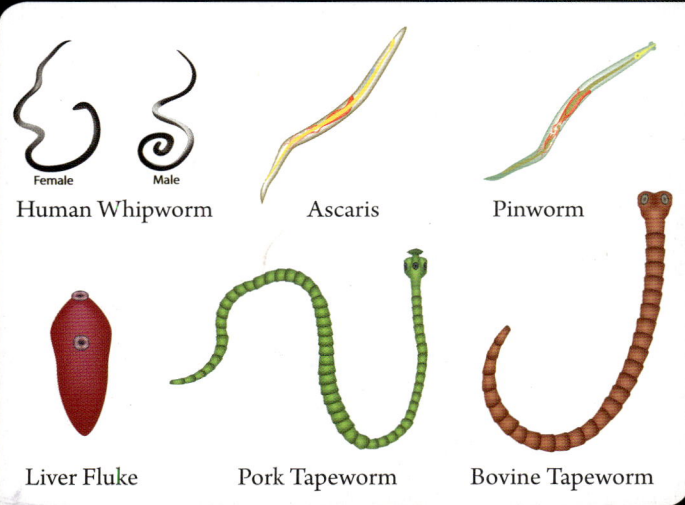

※ *Types of helminths*

GOOD AND BAD BACTERIA

Bacteria are present everywhere, both inside and outside the body. Most bacteria present in the body are harmless and even essential to keep out harmful foreign microbes and maintain good health. There are also many bacterial species that can cause serious illnesses and diseases in humans.

❋ *Good bacteria are present in yogurt and other probiotic food*

Bacteria for Health

Some bacterial species are found in the respiratory tract, skin, intestine, and mouth and usually do not cause any harm. In fact, these organisms that reside in our body are the first line of defense against "foreign" microbes that can potentially be pathogenic (disease-causing). Any imbalance in the normal microbiota can compromise health.

Bacteria and Immunity

Bacteria act like the "tuning forks" of our body's immune response system. Our immunity has to be pitched just right. It should neither be too sensitive nor too slow to react. If and when pathogens infect the body, the immune system should react immediately to eliminate the threat.

Every individual has a unique collection of microbes in their body, collectively referred to as "microbiome". Humans begin acquiring different bacterial species after being born and continue to accumulate them from the environment as they grow. Some bacterial species will take up permanent residence in various parts of the body and become a part of the body's normal population and together aid in the development of a healthy immune system. In a nutshell, the presence of good bacteria curbs the growth of bad bacteria that enter the body through different means.

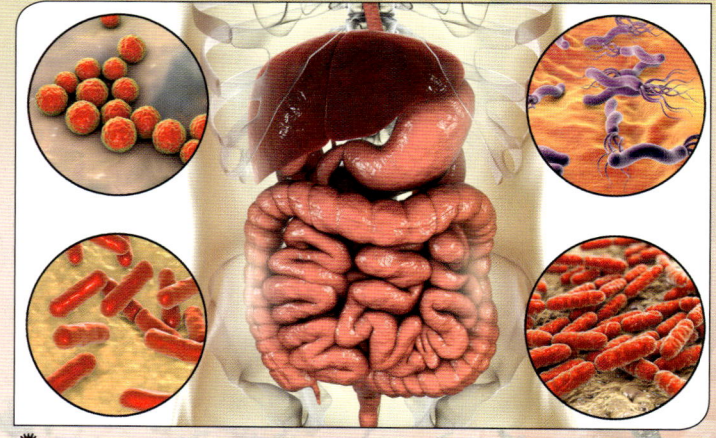

❋ *The intestine's microbiome*

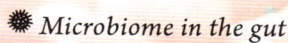

❋ *Microbiome in the gut*

Bacteria that cause Diseases

Diseases usually only happen when the normal microbiota is disrupted for any reason. The use of antibiotics can destroy the good bacteria along with the pathogens and it might take time for the normal population to be restored. The body often houses small populations of bad bacteria without causing any harm. However, when the bad bacteria population increases, it can create an environment that causes disease. For instance, Klebsiella pneumonia population is normally present in the stomach without causing any ill-effects. However, when the Klebsiella population is not kept under check by the normal good bacteria, it can cause colitis (inflammation of colon) and even colorectal cancer.

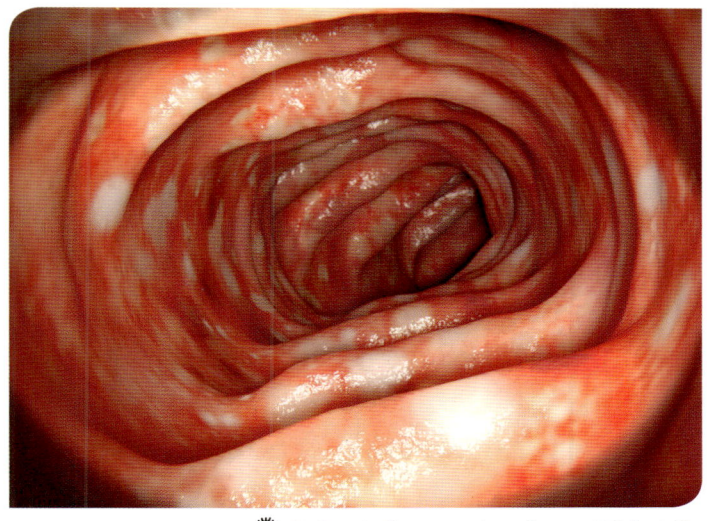

Colon inflammation due to Klebsiella

Effect of Sanitisation

In an effort to make homes and the environment cleaner, people use a range of disinfectants and antiseptics to wipe out microbes. However, studies reveal that making the environment free of bacteria is counterintuitive and instead of reducing incidences of disease, it has instead led to an increase in obesity, cancer, and heart disease.

Research aims at developing antibiotics that target only pathogens without disturbing the good bacteria. Probiotics containing good bacteria cultures and dietary supplements that preserve gut bacteria are prescribed for health benefits.

Overuse of antiseptics and hand sanitizers can also be harmful

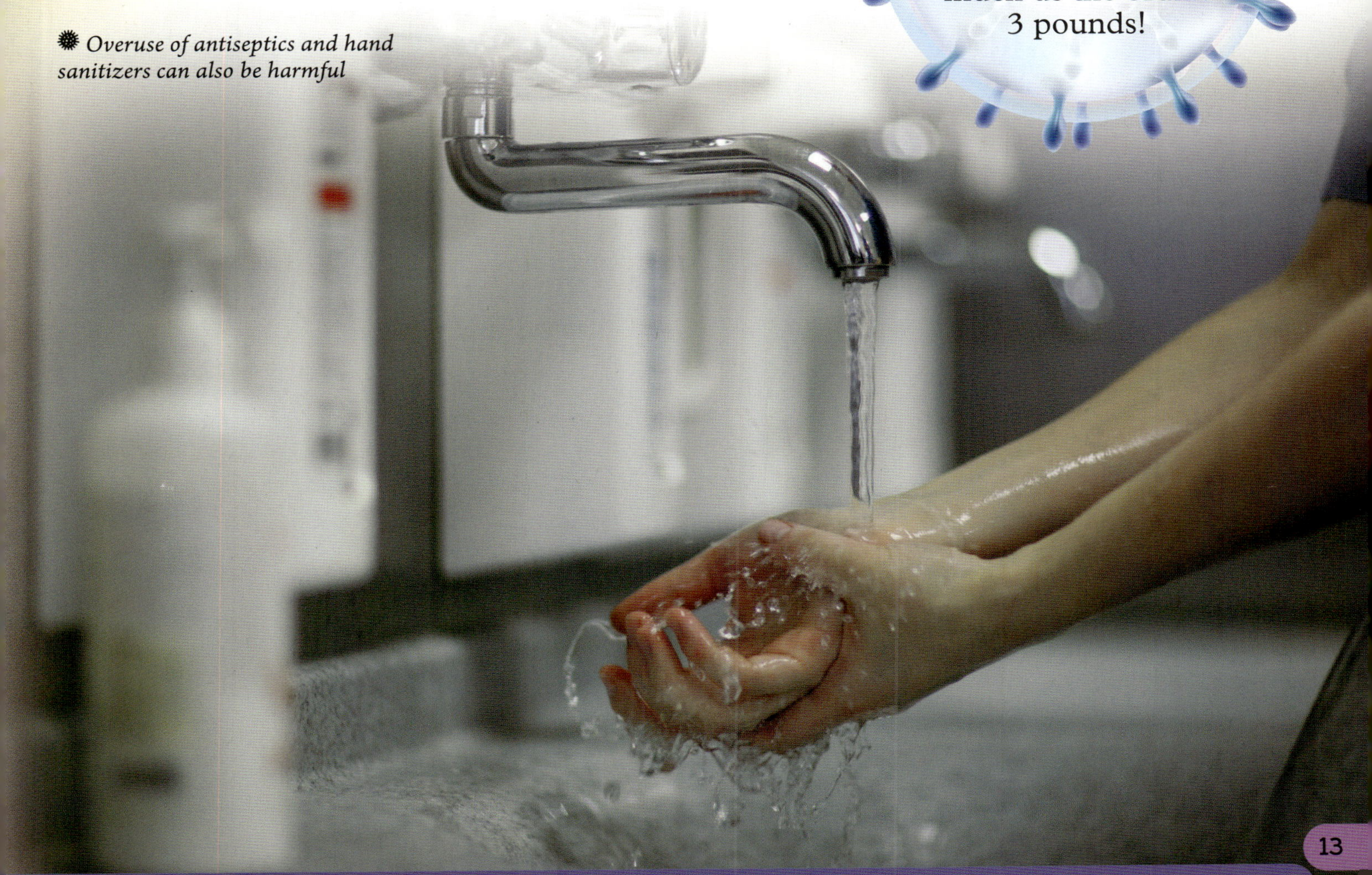

Fact File

On an average, the amount of bacteria present in the body weighs as much as the brain: 3 pounds!

BACTERIAL HABITATS

Bacteria coexist with humans in a balanced yet unique relationship. On one hand, certain bacterial species cause the most dangerous and potentially fatal diseases. On the other hand, several species coexist inside the body while remaining harmless or even essential for maintaining good health.

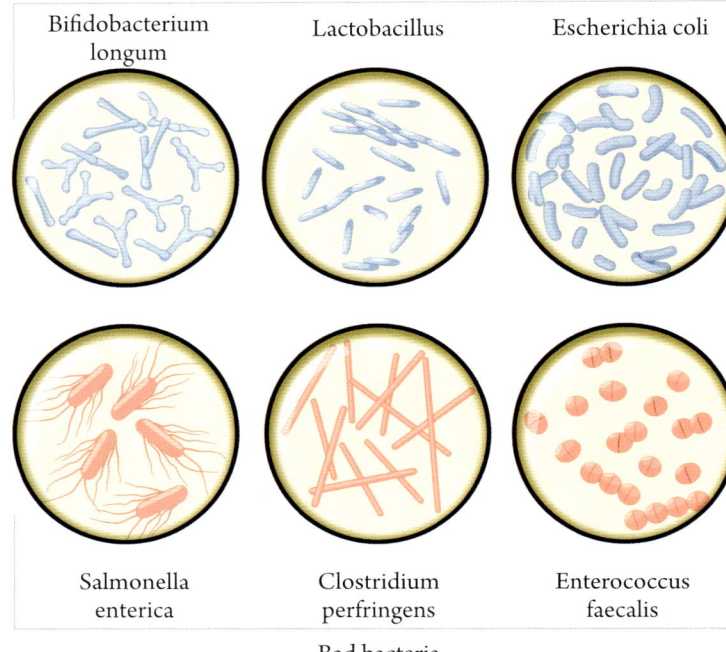

Good vs. bad bacteria

Types of Bacteria

Staphylococcus: Staphylococcus epidermis and Staphylococcus aureus are commonly found in the skin, throat, mouth, and nose. Around 25% of the healthy human population have them. However, infection from some other person's Staphylococcus species can cause skin or ear infection or pneumonia.

Klebsiella: Klebsiella species are found in the intestine and exist harmlessly. Infection from other species in sick patients can cause a variety of serious illnesses ranging from pneumonia and skin or blood infection to meningitis.

Enterococcus: The species are usually found in the intestines, mouth, throat, and urinary tract. An increase in the population due to disruption in normal microbiota can cause urinary tract or blood infections.

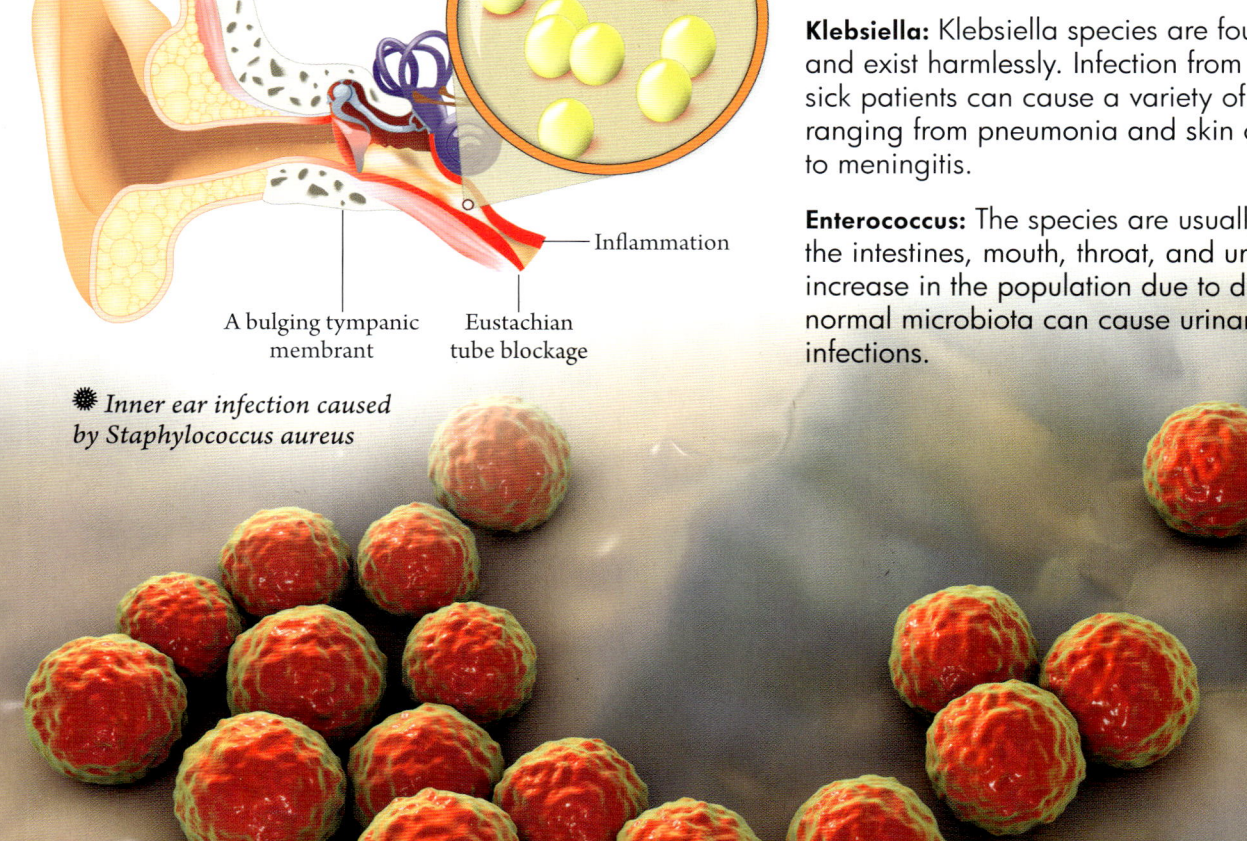

Inner ear infection caused by Staphylococcus aureus

Enterococcus bacteria

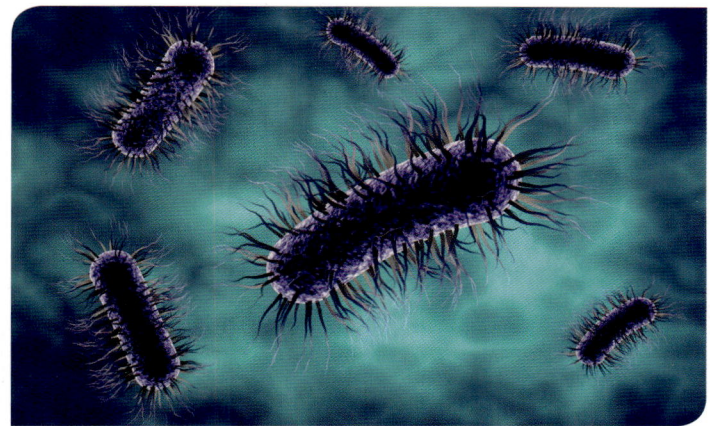

Escherichia coli bacteria

Escherichia coli: This is a diverse bacterial family with many sub species. It is commonly found in the intestine and also in the surroundings. Some species can cause diarrhea or respiratory illnesses.

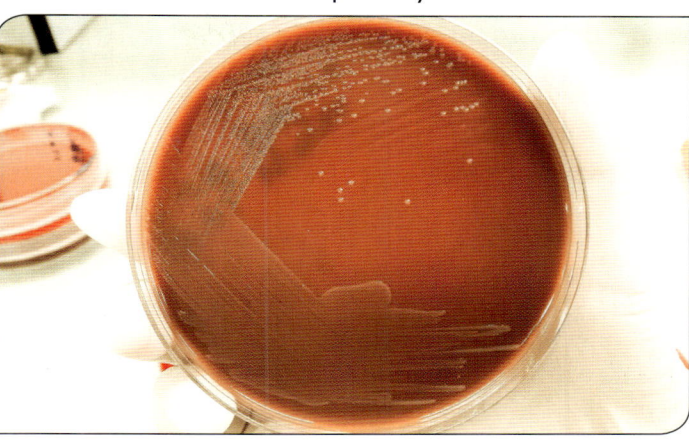

Hemophilus influenzae colonies

Hemophilus: Found commonly in humans, Hemophilus influenzae was originally thought to be responsible for pandemic flu outbreaks. However, most species don't cause any disease unless the immune system is weakened. In such cases, the bacteria multiply rapidly and infect heart valves and respiratory tracts.

Fact File
Lactobacillus lacti, a species commonly found in the body, is also responsible for fermenting milk.

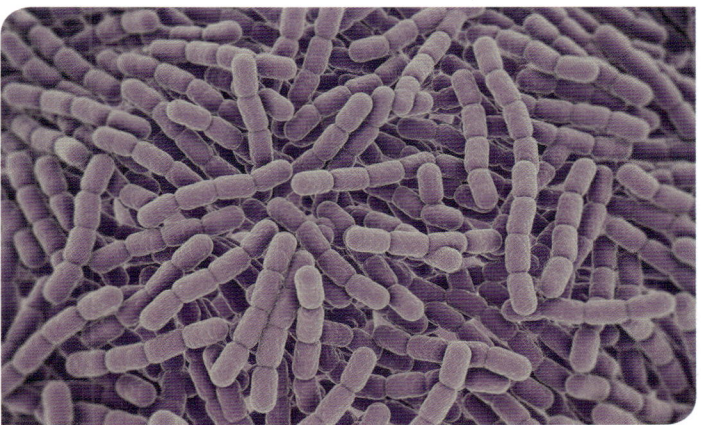

Streptococci live in the form of chains

Bacteroides: Bacteroides species has a complex relationship with humans. When they are present only in the gut, they are useful in assisting in digestion and producing energy. However, when they escape from the intestine and enter into the blood, they can cause severe blood infections.

Clostridium: A few species of Clostridium thrive inside human intestines and also in the soil without causing any problem. However, other strains such as Clostridium tetani and Clostridium botulinum can cause serious and life-threatening infections.

Streptococcus: This common species is found on human skin and in the mouth and throat. Most strains classified under Group A live without causing harm and only cause minor throat or skin infections when they multiply recklessly. Group B species, on the other hand, are capable of causing more serious diseases, especially in new born babies or sick, elderly adults.

Pseudomonas species: Pseudomonas species are versatile and extremely well adapted to survive in a wide range of environments including water, soil, and the human body. They seldom cause infections except in the case of individuals with compromised immunity.

Neisseria: Several species of Neisseria live in humans without causing any harm. They are generally found in the respiratory tract. Only two species are pathogenic – Neisseria gonorrhea and Neisseria meningitidis. Neisseria gonorrhea is never part of the normal flora.

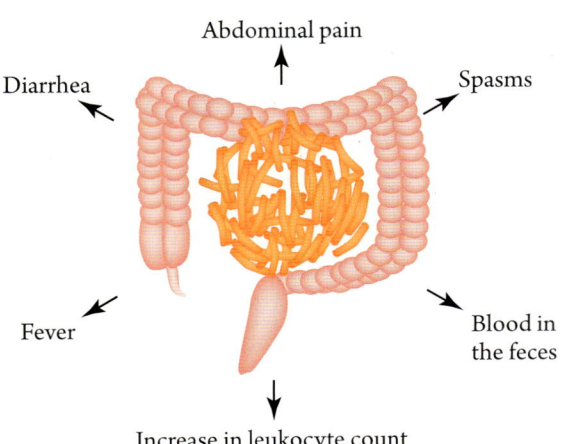

Clostridium difficile infection

BACTERIAL DISEASES

Not all bacterial strains are harmful to us and most species are, in fact, beneficial. Those that can infect and cause disease are called "pathogenic bacteria". Even though there are thousands of bacterial species, very few (less than a hundred) cause diseases. In comparison, several thousand species reside in the digestive system without causing harm.

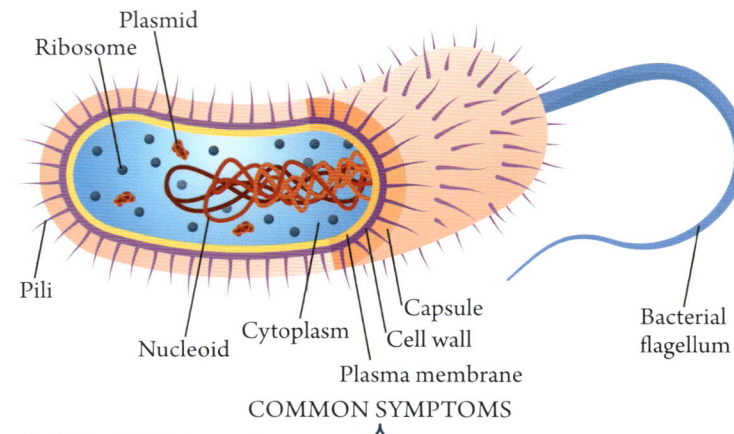

Tuberculosis and Other Major Diseases

Mycobacterium tuberculosis, which causes the disease tuberculosis, is one of the most dangerous bacterial strains. It causes about 2 million deaths every year, the major portion of which occur in sub-Saharan Africa. In 70% of the cases, it affects the lungs. People who have weak immune systems are particularly susceptible.

Other major bacterial diseases include pneumonia, tetanus, typhoid, cholera, syphilis, diphtheria, and leprosy. Most of these diseases are preventable with the help of vaccines and booster doses administered to children right from birth.

COMMON SYMPTOMS

Watery Diarrhea | Nausea and Vomiting | Dehydration

SEVERE SYMPTOMS

 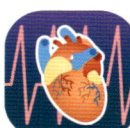  

Muscle cramps | Rapid heart rate | Low blood pressure | Persistent vomiting

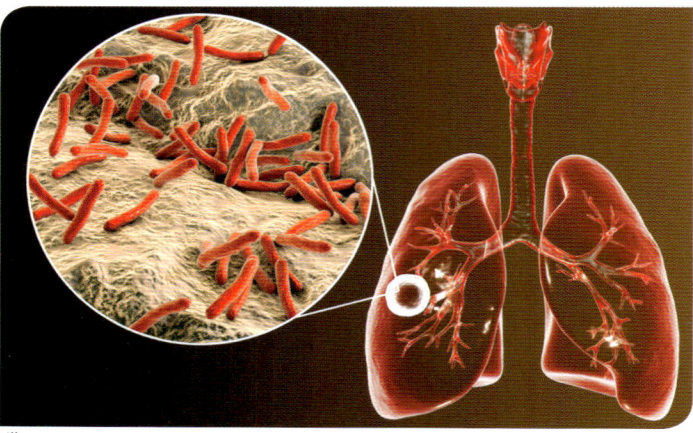

❇ *Tuberculosis causing species – Mycobacterium*

❇ *Symptoms of a bacterial disease: Cholera*

Fact File
According to World Health Organisation (WHO), about one quarter of the world's population is infected with tuberculosis bacteria.

❇ *How tuberculosis spreads*

Bacterial Infection – How It Works

The symptoms of a bacterial disease appear when it damages host tissue or when it interferes with normal organ function. Apart from damaging tissue directly, bacteria can also induce the immune system to react in the form of many symptoms including increased body temperature and swelling of lymph nodes in the neck or armpits.

Bacteria gain entry into the body through different routes such as cuts in the skin, eating contaminated food or water, and contact with others who have a contagious disease. Opportunistic pathogens infect only when the immunity is significantly lowered.

Several bacterial species are capable of living inside cells and are called obligate intracellular parasites. They do not cause disease immediately but only after sufficient incubation inside the cell. Chlamydia and Rickettsia are examples.

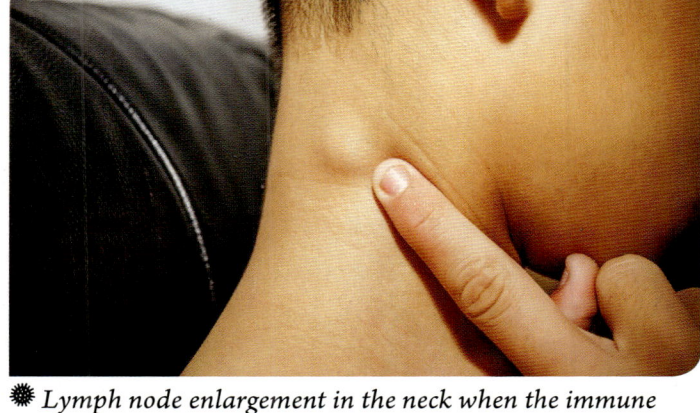
❂ *Lymph node enlargement in the neck when the immune cells are fighting infection*

Treatment and Prevention

Antibiotics are the most important course of treatment for bacterial infections. They can be "bactericidal", capable of destroying pathogenic strains or "bacteriostatic", capable of preventing pathogen growth. Some antibiotics are very specific in action: for instance, tetracycline is capable of inhibiting function of the bacterial ribosome (a cell organelle involved in protein synthesis) but not human ribosome.

The continuous and indiscriminate use of antibiotics can result in antibiotic resistance. Antibiotic resistance occurs when the bacteria are capable of modifying certain physical characteristics to avoid being targeted by one or more antibiotics.

The use of disinfectants and antiseptics as well as sterilisation, especially in hospitals, has been helpful in preventing the spread of different bacterial infections.

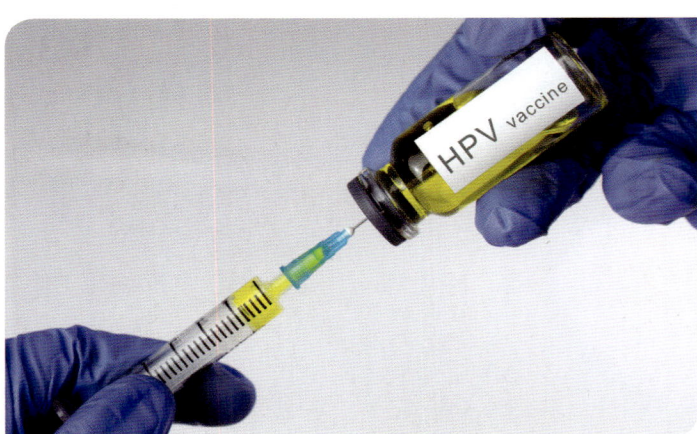
❂ *Vaccines prevent serious diseases*

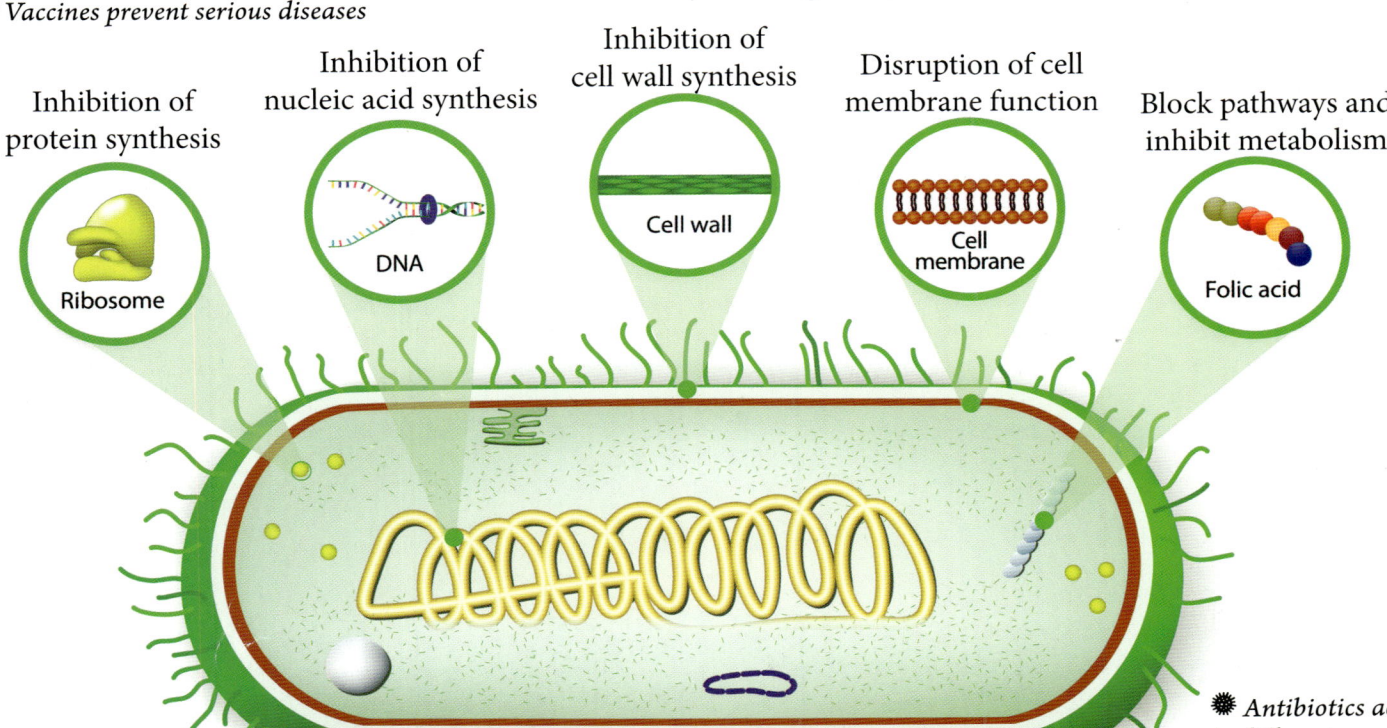
❂ *Antibiotics act in different ways on bacteria*

PROTOZOA

Protozoa are extremely diverse including a wide range of species and are often difficult to classify. They are classified under the sub kingdom of Protista. There are over 65,000 protozoan species, most of which are free-living and capable of thriving in most habitats but most often in soil and water.

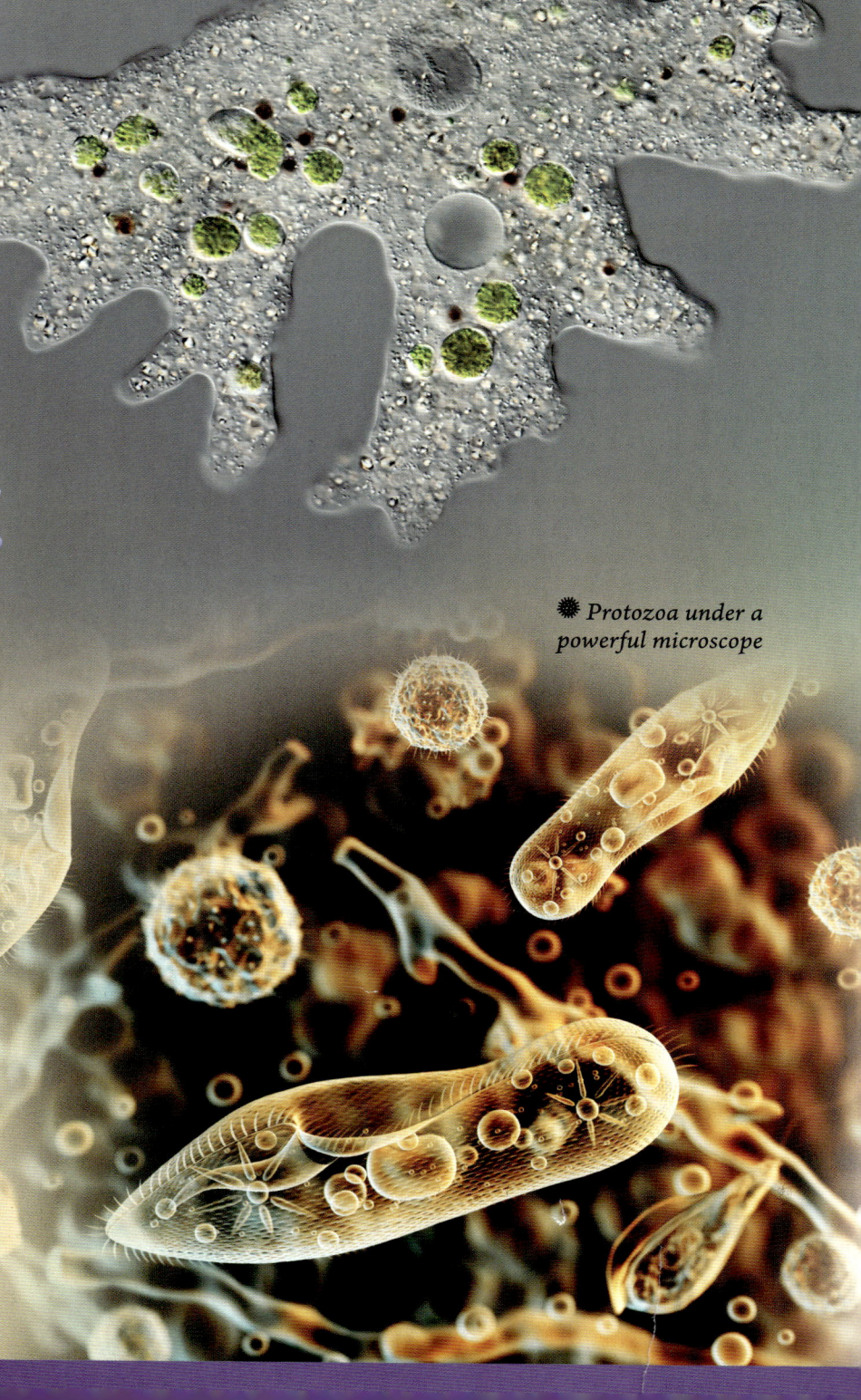

✸ Amoeba is the most well-known protozoan species

Fact File
Malaria, one of the major diseases in tropical countries, is caused by a protozoan called Plasmodium.

✸ Protozoa under a powerful microscope

Classification of Protozoa

Free-living protozoa occur in a variety of habitats. Based on microscopic studies, the species is classified under six major phyla. Most protozoa that cause disease are classified under two of these six phyla: Apicomplexa and Sarcomastigophora. The free-living protozoa are not of any concern to human health as long as they do not gain entry into the body. This is because these species do not directly depend upon another organism for their survival. However, when introduced into the body, they grow, multiply, and cause disease and its associated symptoms.

Protozoa and Nutrition

Protozoa are classified as autotrophs or heterotrophs based on whether or not they are able to manufacture their own food. Euglena and Volvox are two protozoan species that are photoautotrophic, that is, they are capable of manufacturing their own food from sunlight like plants. They are also heterotrophic when there is no sunlight available. In such situations, they obtain nutrition from carbon sources such as acetates, fatty acids, and alcohols.

Most protozoa are purely heterotrophs and depend on different types of diet. Some protozoa feed on bacteria while others feed on algae and phytoplankton. These two types are called microbivores and herbivores respectively.

❂ *Euglena, a photosynthetic protozoa species*

Parasitic protozoa depend on a vertebrate or invertebrate host to multiply. A parasitic protozoan might live in the soil but have the essential components to thrive and multiply in a host when needed. Different species of Amoeba, Trypanosoma, Giardia, and Plasmodium cause diseases in humans. They are often spread through contaminated food or water as well as through the bites of insects.

Feeding and Movement

Among the free-living protozoa there are those that have large, whip-like flagella or short, hair-like cilia for movement and a mouth for entry of food, and others that lack flagella or mouth-like structures. Amoeba, for instance, does not have a mouth or flagella. It moves by extending its "pseudopodia" or false feet. Thus, amoeba doesn't have a fixed shape. The same pseudopodia are also used for engulfing and ingesting food.

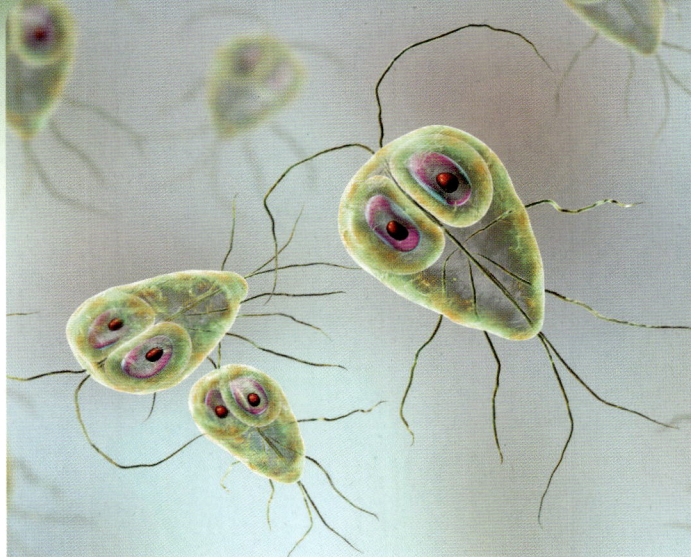

❂ *Giardia, a protozoan parasite that targets the intestines*

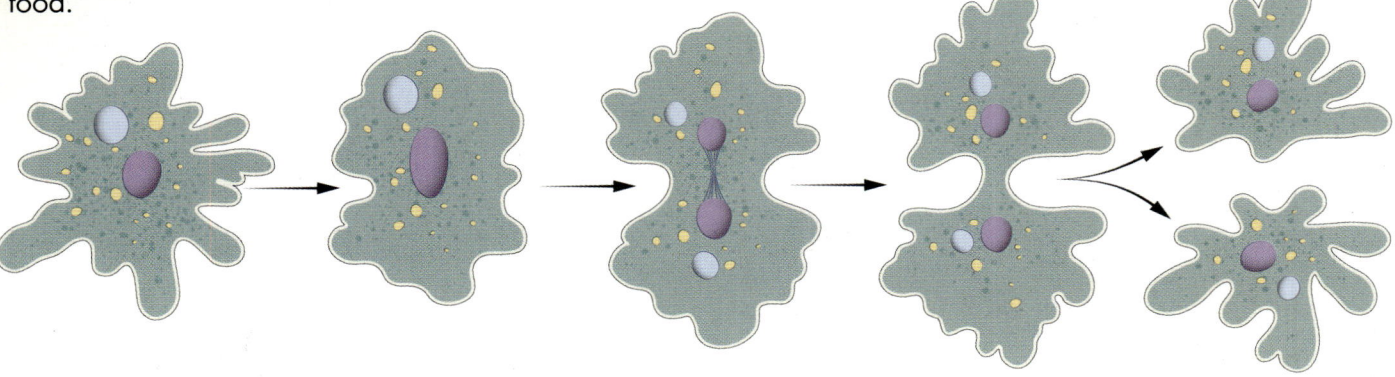

Parent cell | Pseudopodia are pulled in | Nucleus divides | Cytoplasm divides | Two daughter cells

❂ *Movement and reproduction in amoeba*

PROTOZOAN DISEASES

Different protozoan species cause diseases of varying intensity. Among the most common protozoan diseases are amoebiasis, trypanosomiasis, leishmaniasis, trichomoniasis, toxoplasmosis and malaria. Protozoan infections can also cause diarrhea and dysentery.

Amoebiasis: The disease is caused by Entamoeba histolytica. It is also more commonly known as amoebic dysentery. The disease is spread through contaminated drinking water. When the protozoa enter into the body, they penetrate the colon wall, secrete histolytic enzymes that can rupture tissue and result in ulcers and feed on the colon cells. The ulcers rupture and secrete blood and mucus in the intestine that also come out in the stools. Left untreated, the liver, lungs and even the brain can get infected. Houseflies and cockroaches play a role in transmitting the disease if they come in contact with food.

Giardiasis: The flagellate Giardia species is responsible for causing diarrhea. It has sucking discs that helps the parasites attach itself onto epithelial cells of the intestine. This results in malfunction and malabsorption of fat resulting in a variety of symptoms ranging from stomach pain, loss of appetite, headache and allergy apart from diarrhea.

❋ Entamoeba species that causes amoebiasis

Trypanosomiasis: Trypanosomiasis is caused by Trypanosoma species transmitted to humans through blood-sucking insects like mosquitoes and tsetse flies. Trypanosoma is among the most dangerous protozoan parasites. The parasite travels freely in the blood when transmitted through an insect bite and collects in the liver, spleen and lymph glands. When it enters the cerebrospinal fluid it becomes deadly, resulting in coma and death.

❋ Trypanosoma cruzi in the bloodstream

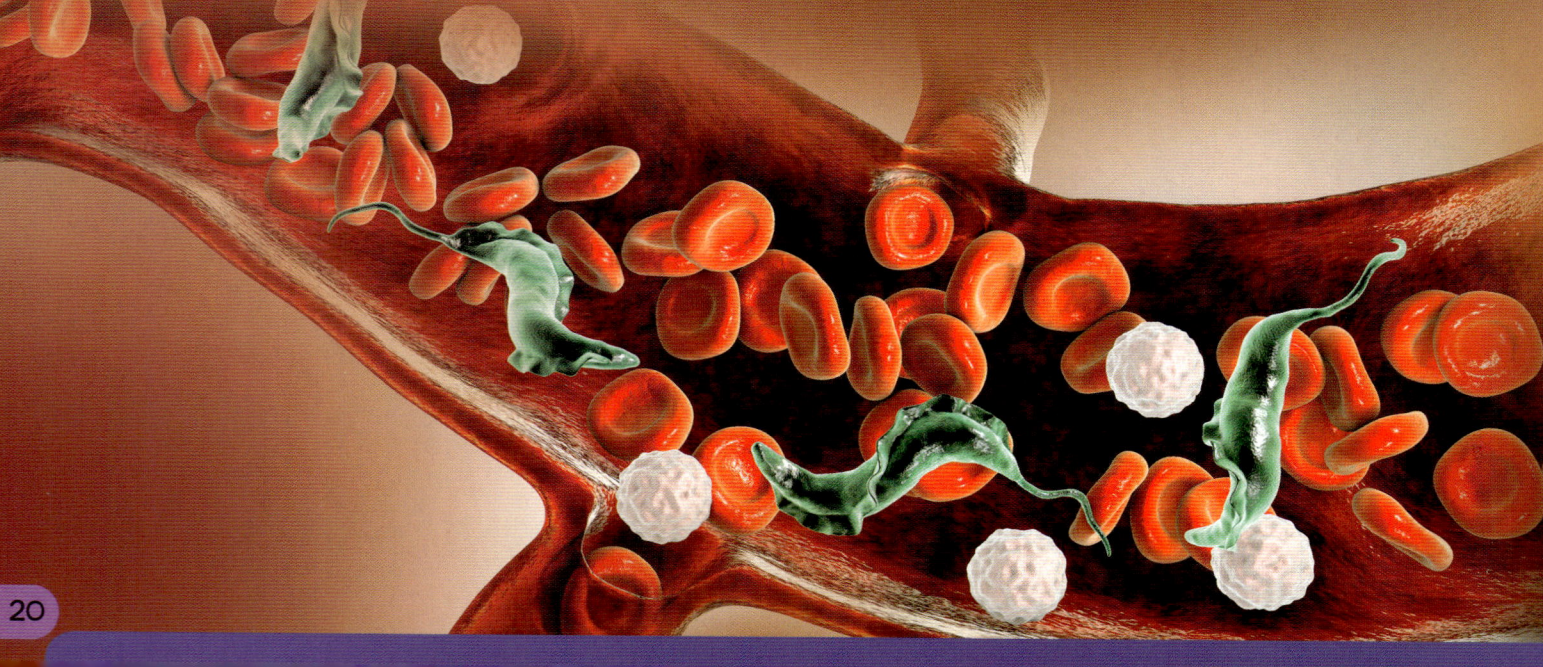

Leishmaniasis: Leishmania is a type of flagellate parasite that is spread through another type of blood-sucking fly called Phlebotomus. The disease caused by one Leishmania species, Leishmania donovani, is called kala-azar. This disease is common in Africa, India, China, South America and Russia. It causes enlargement of vital organs and consequently fever. It causes sores in skin, nasal cavities, mouth and pharynx.

Malaria: Malaria is a disease caused by the parasite Plasmodium, and transmitted through the bite of Anopheles mosquito. Plasmodium species attacks both the liver cells and red blood cells. The parasites release a toxic substance called hemozoin that causes human blood to become watery and results in the various symptoms of malaria. The four common species that cause human malaria include Plasmodium vivax, Plasmodium ovale, Plasmodium falciparum and Plasmodium malaria.

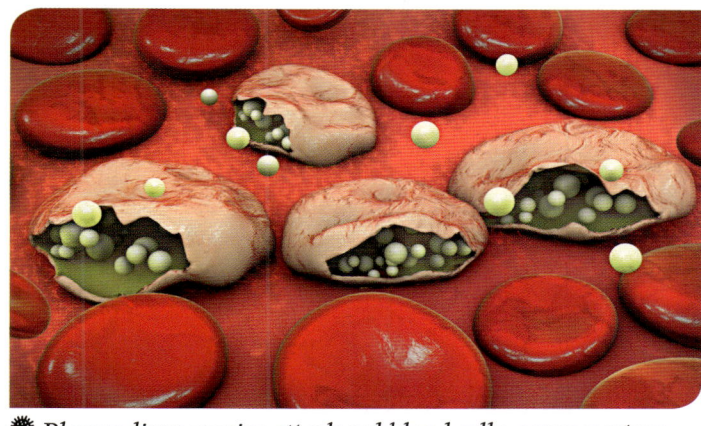

❋ *Plasmodium species attack red blood cells, cause rupture and release of "hemozoin" toxins*

❋ *Toxoplasmosis can be transmitted by cats and transferred to an unborn baby from its mother*

Fact File
Trypanosoma fever is also called "sleeping sickness" and is one of the dangerous diseases in Africa.

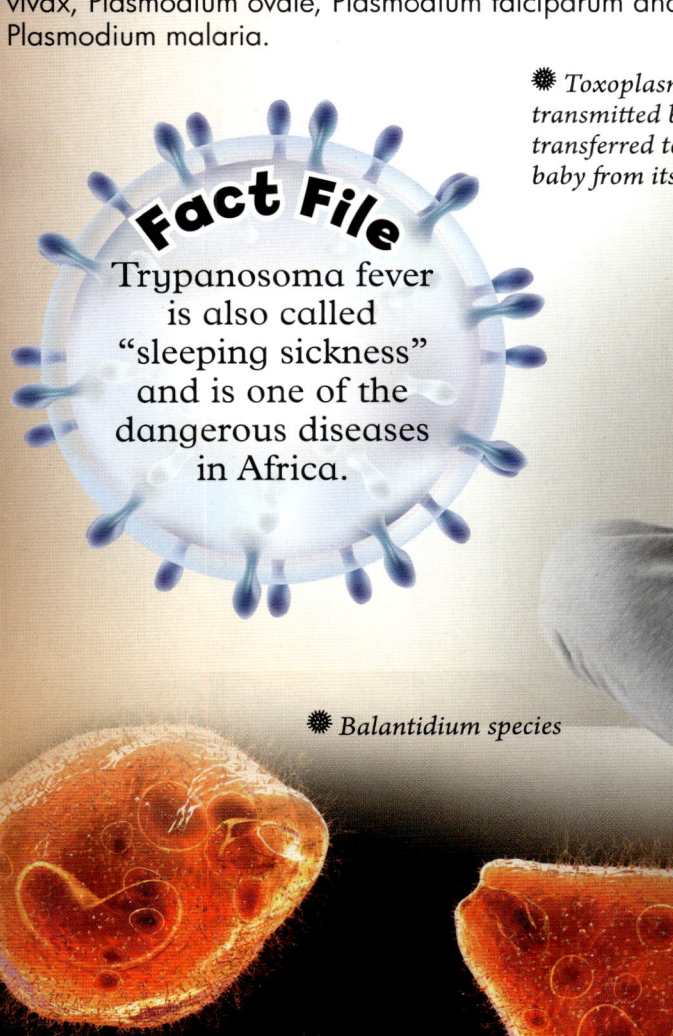

❋ *Balantidium species*

Toxoplasmosis: Caused by the parasite Toxoplasma gondii, the disease occurs when the parasite gains access to the bloodstream. Soon afterwards, it multiplies and spreads to different organs such as brain, spinal cord, lungs, liver, spleen, bone marrow, lymph nodes, heart and skeletal muscles. The disease is often spread through cats.

Balantidial Dysentery: Unlike many other parasitic protozoa with flagella, Balantidium species have short, hair-like cilia instead. They infect the intestine causing ulcers, dysentery and diarrhea.

HELMINTHS

Helminths are parasites that are worm-like and survive by completely depending on hosts for nutrition. Helminths vary in size from less than a millimetre to as long as a metre. All helminths are invertebrates and possess flat, long or round bodies. Humans are among the many different hosts of helminths.

Among the different types of helminths, the most commonly known ones are:

Roundworms: They are slender worms that live and reproduce in the human intestine, entering the body through contaminated food or water or through mosquito bites. They are commonly found in warm and tropical climates. Symptoms of disease appear only after the roundworms multiply and there are larger numbers inside. There are thousands of species of roundworm itself. Giant roundworms are much larger and can measure up to 30 centimetres.

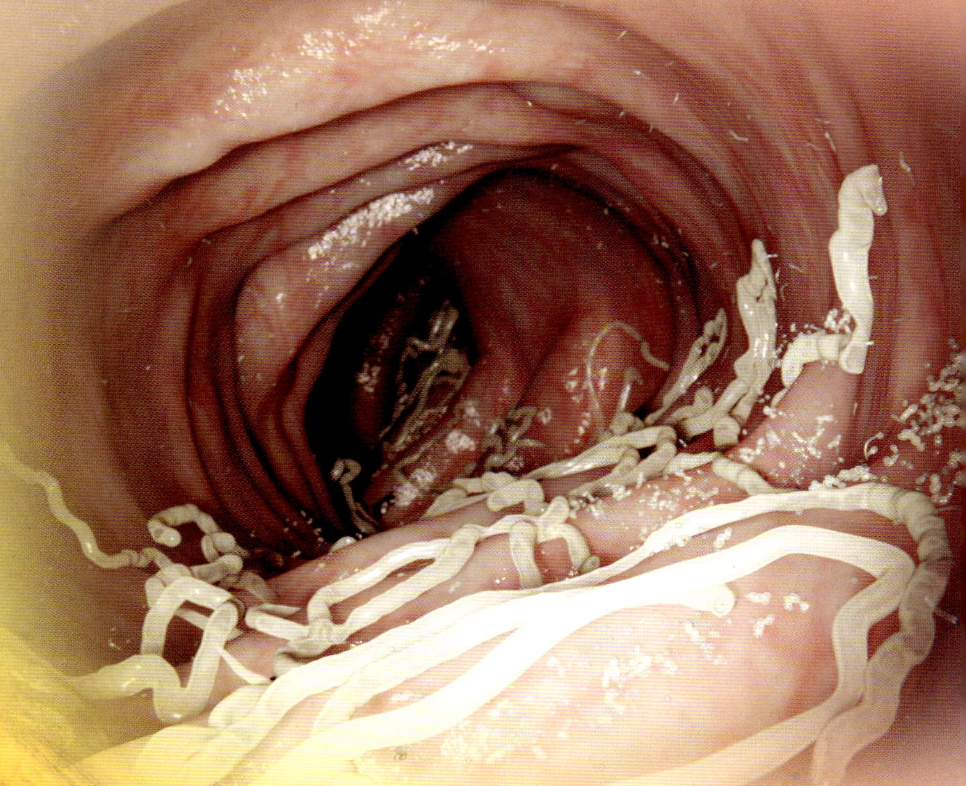

✺ Large roundworms in intestine walls

Whipworms: They earn the name from their distinct "whip-like" shape with a thick tail and tapered front. Trichuris trichiura is the whipworm species that infects humans. Roughly 600 to 800 million people are infected with whipworm.

Hookworms: Greyish white or pink in colour, the hookworm has a head that is bent at an angle and hence resembles a hook. The distinct feature of this worm is its mouthpart, equipped with cutting plates instead of teeth to latch onto intestine walls. They are smaller than roundworms and consequently cause less tissue destruction. Walking barefoot in the soil where they are present can cause them to latch onto the skin and enter into the body.

✺ Whipworm with its characteristic whip-like tail

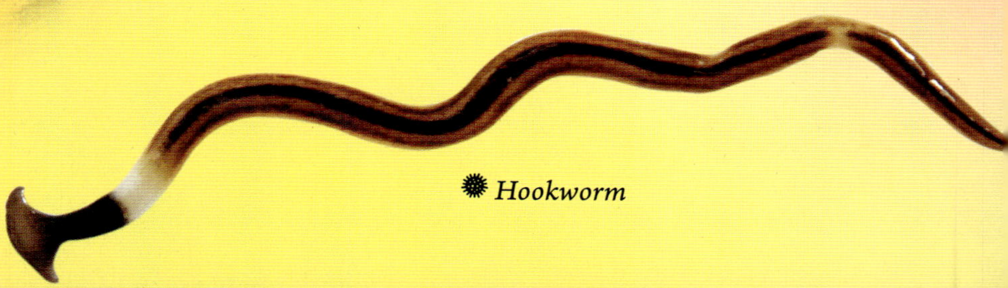

✺ Hookworm

Filarial worms: Wuchereria bancrofti is a species of Filarial worm transmitted to humans through mosquito bites. The worms reside in the lymph nodes often causing painful fluid accumulation and swelling in the limbs.

Tapeworms: Tapeworms are flat and ribbon-like in appearance and enter the intestines through contaminated, raw pork, beef or fish. Since tapeworms absorb Vitamin B12, they cause the symptoms of Vitamin B12 deficiency including depression, mouth ulcers and yellow tinged skin.

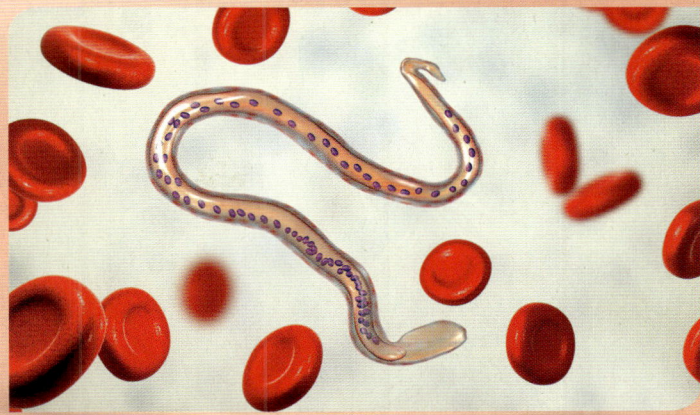

✹ *Wuchereria bancrofti that causes Filariasis*

✹ *Close-up of tapeworm*

Fact File
Helminths are a major concern in developing countries, above malaria and TB, with more than two billion people affected!

Flukes: Flukes are leaf-shaped worms that are classified as tissue flukes or blood flukes. Tissue flukes infect liver, bile ducts or other tissues. In the tissues, the flukes feed slowly on the epithelial cells. Blood flukes reside in the blood in one part of their lifecycle and cause a variety of symptoms. It becomes dangerous when the flukes gain access to vital organs such as lungs or brain and can cause long-term damage.

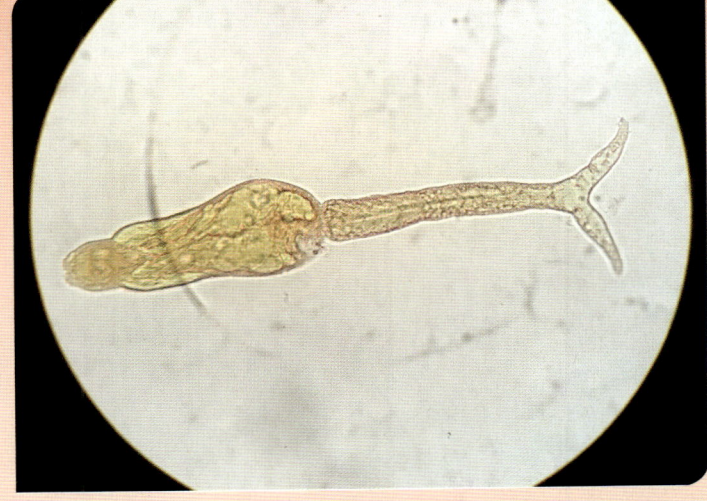

✹ *Blood fluke seen under the microscope*

HELMINTHIC DISEASES

Infections caused by parasitic helminths are generally referred to as worm infections. The most common helminths that attack humans include roundworms, tapeworms and flukes. Most helminths prefer to reside in the intestinal tract absorbing nutrients easily. However, some can also burrow into other organs and cause significant tissue damage.

Helminthic Parasites in Soil

Most helminths are found in warm and humid tropical regions, often present in the soil and transmitted to humans through accidental ingestion. Helminthic diseases transmitted through the soil have resulted in a number of ailments including malnutrition, organ damage and anemia. Helminthiasis is a leading problem in countries with poor sanitation and poverty.

❋ Swimming in contaminated ponds or pools can cause helminth infection

❋ Close-up of dog roundworm

Infection by Helminths

Helminthic diseases are caused by three major categories of parasites: roundworms, also known as nematodes, tapeworms and flukes.

Filariasis: These parasites hatch and thrive in the intestine and either remain there or travel to other parts of the body. Generally, the symptoms of roundworm infection causes fatigue, diarrhea, abdominal pain, fever and itching. Filariasis is a disease caused by roundworms spread by mosquitoes and black flies. It is characterized by abnormal swelling and thickening of skin in the leg and hence referred to as "elephantiasis".

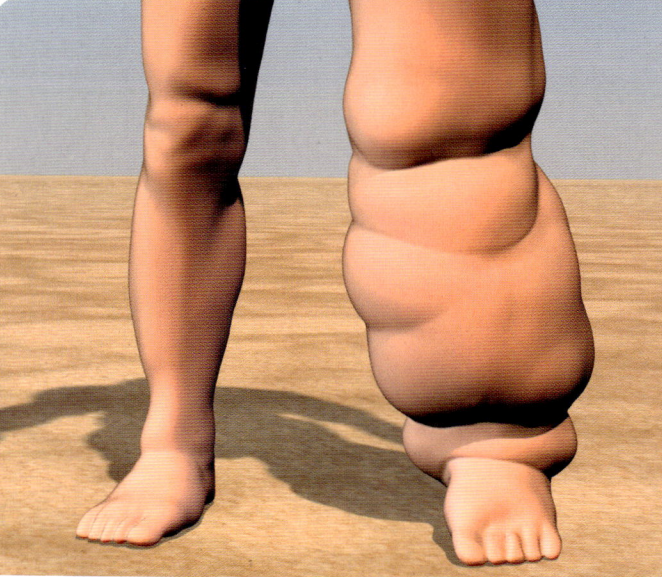
❋ Abnormal swelling of leg

Diarrhea: Like roundworms, tapeworms reside in the intestines, often entering the system through raw, uncontaminated meat consumption. Abdominal pain, diarrhea and fatigue are the common symptoms of tapeworm infection.

Organ Infection: Flukes reside in different parts of the body such as the liver, lungs, spleen and intestine. Freshwater snails play an important role in transmitting the flukes to humans upon contact. In severe cases, flukes can even infect the brain and spinal cord.

❋ *Tapeworm in intestine*

Fact File
There are over 300 known helminths that are capable of infecting humans and causing different diseases.

❋ *Freshwater snails can spread flatworms to humans*

Snail fever: Snail fever or bilharzia is caused by flatworms called "schistosomes". The parasites are spread to humans through contact with freshwater snails.

Treatment and Cure

While there are drugs available for different helminthic diseases, there is no one cure that works for all. While some diseases are easy to cure within days through drugs, others take much longer, even months or years. Some diseases inflict permanent damage to organs or limbs. The best way to prevent infection is to maintain sanitation and avoid contaminated or uncooked food, especially meat. It is also important to be cautious while using public swimming pools and drinking water that can be contaminated with liver flukes.

❋ *Liver fluke*

FUNGI

Fungi comprise a large and diverse group of organisms that are heterotrophic, that is, they absorb nutrition from decomposing organic matter or other hosts. Mushrooms and mold as well as microscopic yeast and other parasitic species fall under this diverse group of organisms. Skin cuts and wounds are the common entry points for parasitic fungi.

Fungi and the Food Industry

There are many beneficial fungal species that have been employed by humans for hundreds of years. Among the many uses of fungi, the most prominent and well-recognized is the role of yeast in bread-making and fermentation. Saccharomyces cerevisiae, or baker's yeast, is a key component of bread and wine production.

Roquefort cheese has its unique pungent flavor because of the mixture of a Penicillium species added into the curd. The fungi multiply and result in blue veins and the characteristic taste for which it is valued.

✸ *Dermatitis caused by fungal species*

✸ *Baker's yeast and bread products*

* *Edible mushrooms*

Many mushroom species are edible while others secrete toxic compounds and hence are dangerous. Edible mushrooms are cultivated in mushroom farms and sold to supermarkets and stores.

Magic mushrooms contain a key ingredient called "psilocybin", which gets converted in the body into psilocin. This compound acts as a psychedelic drug that can cause changes in mood, thoughts, and perception and induce hallucination. While these "shrooms" are not banned, their sale is not legal.

* *Penicillin, an important drug for treating bacterial diseases*

Fungal Antibiotics

Serious bacterial infections and their dangers were a reality until the discovery of Penicillium species by Alexander Fleming and the invention of the Penicillin antibiotic that revolutionized the field of medicine in the 20th century. There are several fungal species that naturally produce antibiotic compounds against different bacterial species.

Fact File
Portobello, shiitake, crimini, white, oyster, and truffle are some of the different types of edible mushrooms.

* *Mold in the walls*

Mold and Fungal Parasites

Among the fungal species that destroy food include the black and white mold with distinctive spore heads and stalks visible to the naked eye. They are commonly found in moist bread, fruits and vegetables and make the food unfit for consumption. Unknowingly ingesting mold can cause a variety of symptoms.

There are many fungal parasites including Candida, Aspergilla and a few other species that are more or less harmless in people with a strong immune system. People with weak or compromised immunity are susceptible to infection by one or more fungal species.

FUNGAL DISEASES

There are more than 1.5 million fungal species identified so far. Only a small fraction, about 300 species, are capable of causing disease. Fungal diseases are classified as systemic, subcutaneous, or superficial depending on where the infection occurs and how deep it is. They are easy to treat and can be completely cured when diagnosed in their early stages.

✸ *Close-up of mold spores*

✸ *Claviceps purpurea growing in barley*

St. Anthony's Fire

Also more commonly known as "ergotism", this fungal disease is the result of long-term consumption of food contaminated with spores of the fungal species Claviceps purpurea. The spores are most commonly found in cereal grains, especially rye. The symptoms are severe and range from uncontrolled convulsions, nausea, mania, vomiting, to headaches and blisters.

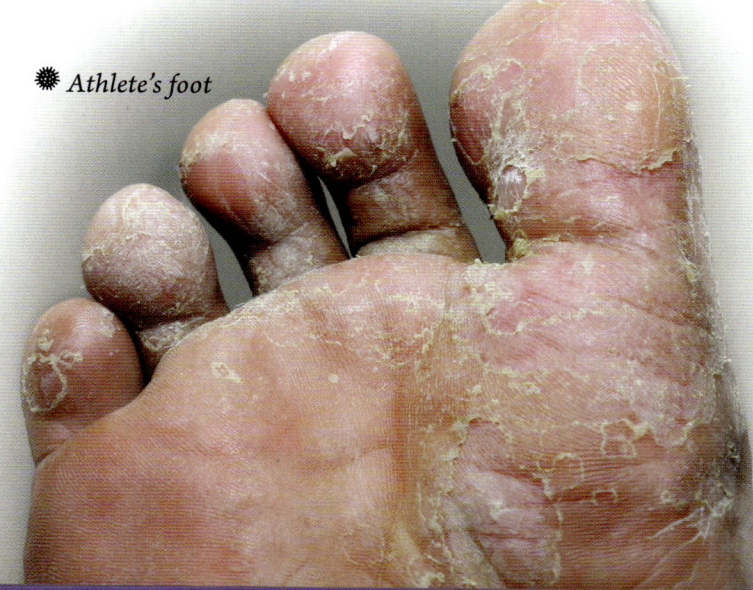

✸ *Athlete's foot*

Ringworm

Ringworm is a common fungal infection caused by a group of fungal species called "dermatophytes". It is called "ringworm" because of the circular rash that develops a ring-like appearance. If left untreated, it can cause severe itching, redness, and spread to other parts of the body. Also, depending on the location, it is referred to by different names. For instance, ringworm on the foot is called "athlete's foot" while in the scalp, it is known as "tinea capitis".

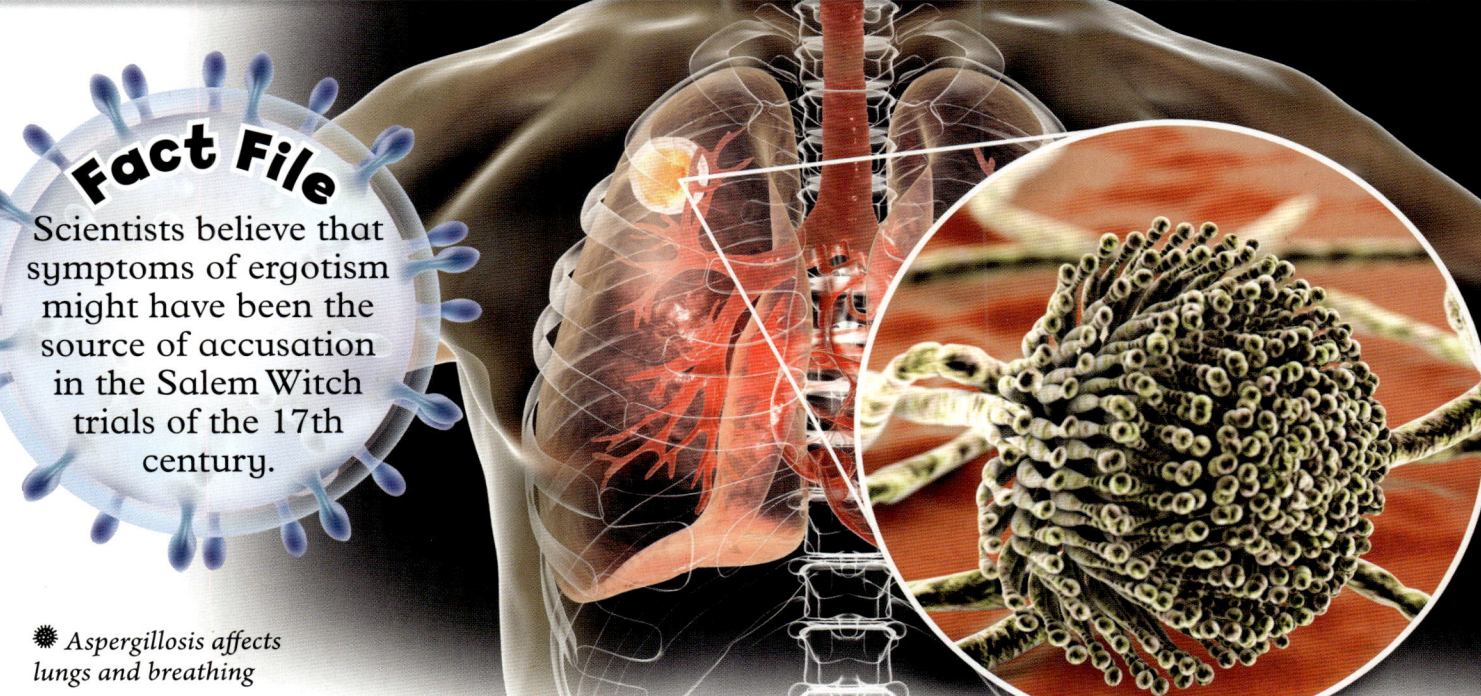

Fact File
Scientists believe that symptoms of ergotism might have been the source of accusation in the Salem Witch trials of the 17th century.

❋ *Aspergillosis affects lungs and breathing*

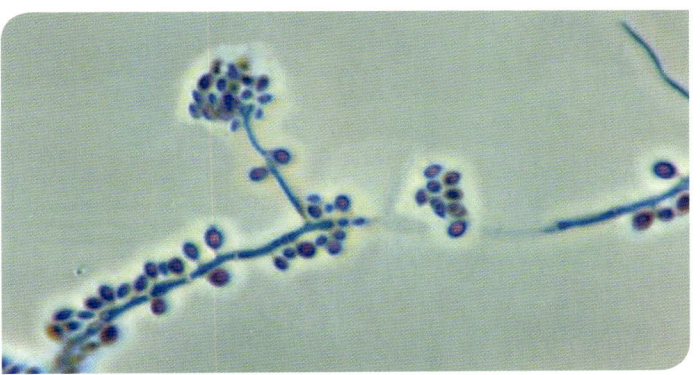

❋ *Microscope view of Sporothrix*

Aspergillosis
This is an infection caused by the inhalation of Aspergillus spores, indoors or outdoors. For most people, this does not lead to any illness as the immune system is effective enough to tackle them. Only those with lung disease or a weak immune system develop allergic reactions and infections in the lungs due to the spores.

Thrush
Candida species are members of the yeast family and are harmless dwellers in the body and cause problems only in an environment that encourages their uncontrolled growth and multiplication. Candidiasis of the mouth and throat is commonly known as "oral thrush". If the infection spreads to the food pipe or esophagus which connects the mouth and stomach, it is known as "candida esophagitis". This is a common problem in people with severely weak immune systems.

Rose Gardener's Disease
This disease, also known as sporotrichosis, is caused by the Sporothrix fungal species. It is found in the soil and plants, particularly rose bushes. When the spores come into contact with open cuts in the skin, sometimes caused by pricking of thorns, they gain entry into the body and cause coughing, chest pain and fever.

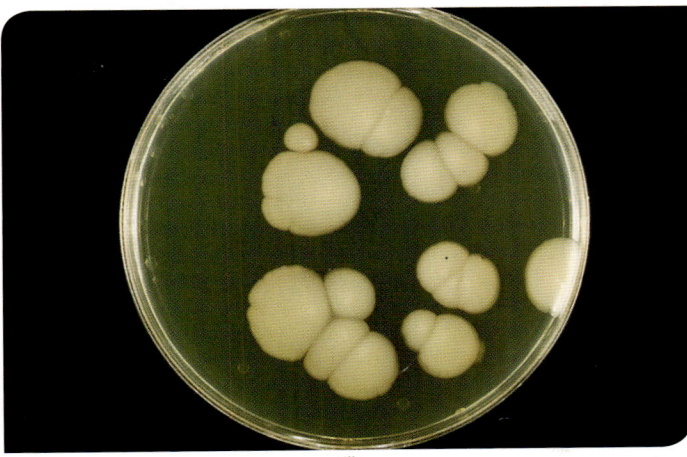

❋ *Candida grown in petri plate*

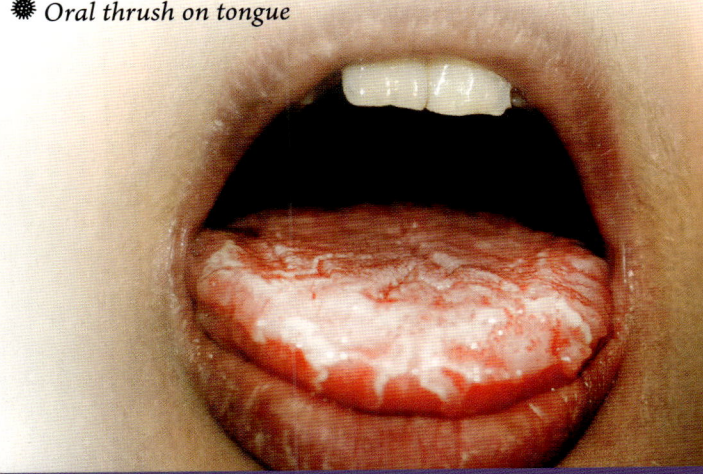

❋ *Oral thrush on tongue*

PARASITIC VECTORS

Some diseases are not directly transmitted from one human to another. Another organism, such as a bird or insect, acts as an intermediary host or "vector" that transmits the disease from an ill individual to a healthy person. Mosquitoes, flies, ticks, mites, and fleas are the most common vectors that transmit diseases.

Vector-Borne Diseases

Did you know that vector-borne diseases make up over 17% of all cases of infectious diseases, causing 700,000 casualties, every year? Malaria, dengue, Chagas disease, leishmaniasis, and schistosomiasis are some of the dangerous parasitic diseases transmitted by vectors.

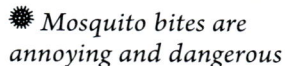
Mosquito bites are annoying and dangerous

The kissing bug spreads Chagas disease

Fact File
Over 90% of serious malaria cases are spotted in sub-Saharan Africa, particularly in the Republic of Congo and Nigeria.

Favorable Conditions for Vectors

Most vectors are blood-sucking insects that bite multiple people. These insects ingest the parasites responsible for causing the disease during a blood meal. The next time they bite someone else, Vector-borne diseases flourish in regions that are thickly populated and have poor sanitation. Mosquitoes, for instance, breed in water. Houses where there is extensive water logging, open sewage, or discarded vessels collecting rain water, provide the ideal environment for mosquitoes to lay eggs and for the larvae to develop.

Blood-fed female laying eggs

Adult emerging — *Life Cycle of the Mosquito.* — Eggs

Pupa — Larva

Stagnant water is a breeding ground for mosquitoes

Vectors and Diseases

Vectors transmit different bacterial and protozoan parasites as well as viruses across hosts. The table shows a list of diseases caused by different vectors:

Insect Vector	Diseases
Aedes mosquito	Dengue, Chikungunya, Yellow fever, Rift Valley fever
Anopheles mosquito	Malaria, Lymphatic Filariasis
Culex mosquito	Lymphatic Filariasis, West Nile fever, Japanese Encephalitis
Sandfly	Sandfly fever, Leishmaniasis
Tsetse fly	Sleeping sickness (African trypanosomiasis)
Black fly	River blindness
Botfly	Myiasis (sores)
Demodex sp. mite	Demodicosis (itch skin rashes)
Tick	Babesiosis
Flea	Bubonic Plague, Typhus

Flea on human skin

A Mosquito's Bite

A mosquito's bite is often undetected except when the immune system reacts to it. When a mosquito bites, it releases its saliva and anti-coagulants (that liquefy blood, thus making it easy to be sucked). While the initial reaction does not elicit a response, the subsequent bite causes itching, redness, and swelling within a day of the bite. A few adults may even become "desensitized" or experience no reaction following a mosquito's bite. When a mosquito transmits the Plasmodium parasite species into the blood, the symptoms appear only after a certain period when the parasites grow and multiply.

Mites can bite and spread disease

Mosquitoes have special mouthparts to suck blood

Flies and Other Vectors

Flies not only play a role in transmitting the parasite to humans but also in the migration of parasitic larvae from the skin to deep inside the tissues. It is possible to avoid picking up eggs or fly larvae by not lying on the ground or drying clothes in open air. Ironing clothes is a great way of destroying any eggs laid on the cloth material.

Ticks, mites, and fleas are found in unhygienic conditions and poorly aired bedding. They can also be transmitted by dogs or cats cohabiting in a small, cramped space.

COMMON MODES OF PARASITE TRANSMISSION

Bacteria, fungi, protozoa and helminths are the common microbes that can infect humans and cause diseases. Different organisms infect in different ways. While Giardia species infest and multiply in the intestine, Paramecium species thrive in the bloodstream. Helminths develop outside in the soil or in another host before they are capable of infecting humans.

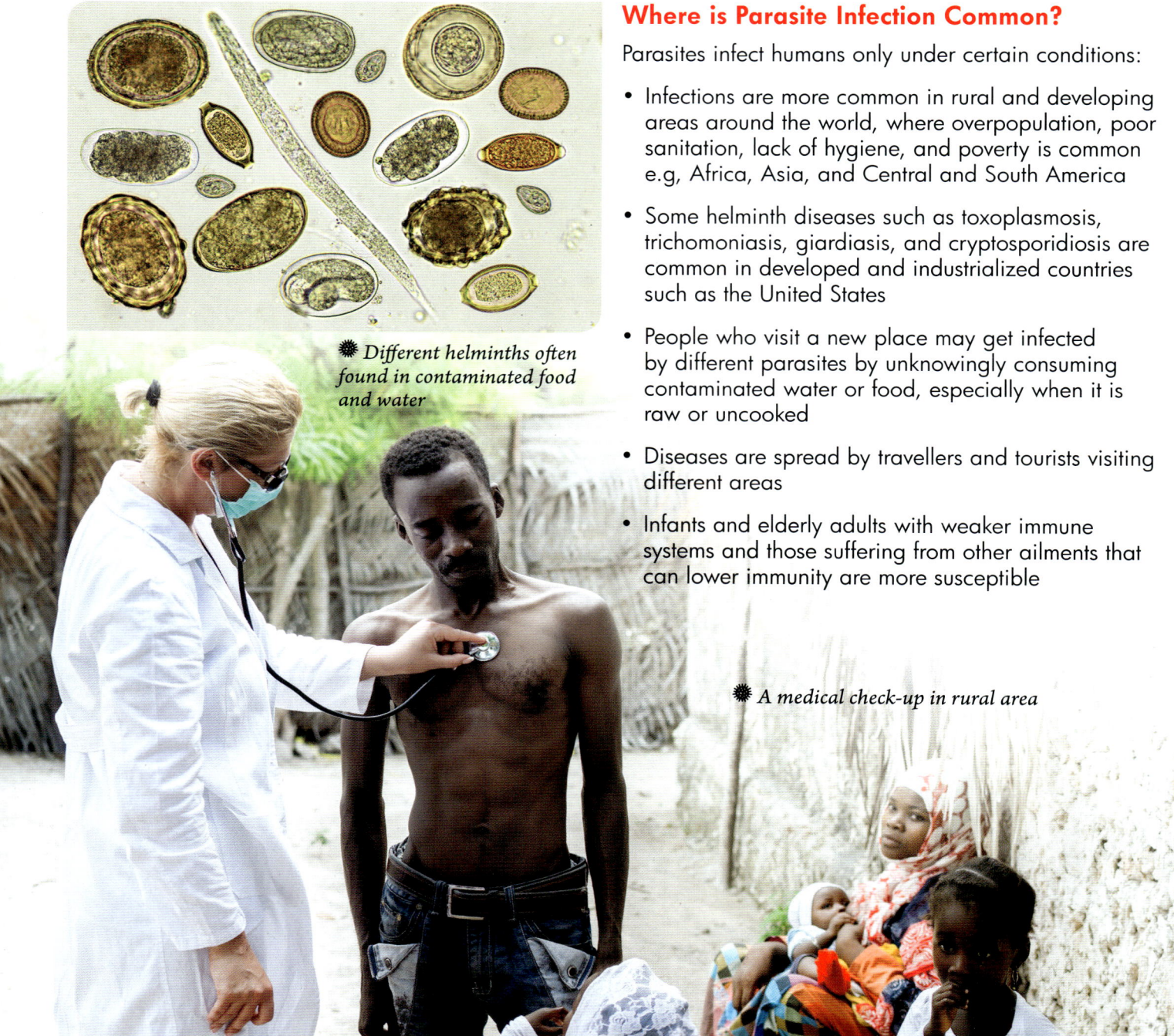

✸ *Different helminths often found in contaminated food and water*

Where is Parasite Infection Common?

Parasites infect humans only under certain conditions:

- Infections are more common in rural and developing areas around the world, where overpopulation, poor sanitation, lack of hygiene, and poverty is common e.g, Africa, Asia, and Central and South America

- Some helminth diseases such as toxoplasmosis, trichomoniasis, giardiasis, and cryptosporidiosis are common in developed and industrialized countries such as the United States

- People who visit a new place may get infected by different parasites by unknowingly consuming contaminated water or food, especially when it is raw or uncooked

- Diseases are spread by travellers and tourists visiting different areas

- Infants and elderly adults with weaker immune systems and those suffering from other ailments that can lower immunity are more susceptible

✸ *A medical check-up in rural area*

Fact File

Hookworms are capable of latching onto and boring into skin, so walking barefoot on contaminated soil can result in transmission.

Modes of Transmission

Parasites commonly enter the body through two main routes: skin and mouth. There are certain parasites that are capable of directly burrowing into the skin upon coming into contact with it. Some parasites enter the intestines by being swallowed in contaminated food or water. There, they are able to attack the intestinal tissue and multiply. A few other parasites are transmitted to humans through insect bites.

In addition to these common routes, parasites can be transmitted to humans through blood transfusion, organ transplantation and mother to fetus transmission.

❋ Raw vegetables and fruits may carry harmful parasites

❋ Meat gets contaminated by parasites and vectors like flies that sit on it

The Fecal-Oral Route of Transmission

The fecal-oral route is the most common mode of parasite transmission. It is a way of transmitting the parasites from the feces of an infected animal or person to another person if they, somehow, consume food or water contaminated with it. Since the parasites are often found in the digestive tract, the eggs or parasites are present in feces. Infection through the fecal-oral route occurs through these common ways:

- Drinking water contaminated with untreated sewage
- Eating raw, contaminated pork or shellfish such as oysters and clams
- Eating raw vegetables and fruits washed in contaminated water
- Swimming in pools or lakes contaminated with parasites
- Physical contact with other contaminated hands

STUDY OF INFECTIOUS DISEASES

Several scientific inventions, factors and people contributed to the study and further understanding of the processes of infection and disease from parasites. This continuous process of gaining knowledge about germs has enabled effective treatment and eradication of diseases.

Fact File
The Ebers papyrus is one of the sources of knowledge about medicines and cures used by ancient Egyptian physicists.

Ancient Egyptians and the Helminth Problems

Studies on the preserved remains and hieroglyphic medical accounts from ancient Egypt reveal that diseases due to parasitic worms were very common. Even though cures for the problems involved non-scientific solutions such as incantations, dung, droppings, and cooked mice, the Egyptians also knew some genuine cures. The root of the pomegranate tree, with its known anti-helminthic properties, was used as a cure thousands of years ago.

❋ *Ebers papyrus*

Hippocrates and Public Health

More than 2500 years ago, Hippocrates, the father of medicine, made a few observations with respect to the effect of climate on health. He believed that people living in different places with unique climates might suffer from different diseases. He also noticed that sudden or abrupt change in weather patterns also affected health conditions and severity of infectious diseases. His study provided early clues on our understanding of the role and prevention of epidemics (or large-scale disease spreading).

❋ *Hippocrates, father of medicine*

Leeuwenhoek and his Microscope

The Danish scientist Anton van Leeuwenhoek, known as the father of microbiology, took special interest in making a variety of lenses that he used for designing microscopes. The microscope helped him, and many others afterwards, look at and understand parasites such as protozoa and bacteria. The development of more advanced microscopes with better resolution paved the way for better analysis and discovery of cures for a wide range of parasite diseases.

❋ *Leeuwenhoek Microscope*

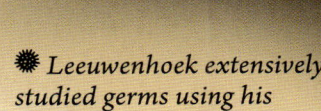

❋ *Leeuwenhoek extensively studied germs using his crude microscopes*

A Cure for Malaria from Bark

As early as the 1600's, a countess who was treated for malaria with the help of the bark of the cinchona tree took the cure back to Europe. In 1820, two French chemists isolated the chemical compound in the bark and called it "quinine". Today, it is still one of the first choices of drug for curing malaria.

❋ *Quinine is isolated from cinchona bark*

Pasteurisation for Safe Milk

Like other uncooked products such as raw meat and egg yolk, milk obtained from cows is also susceptible to a wide range of microbes. In order to come up with a safe and simple way to ensure that milk is free of germs, Louis Pasteur devised a technique called "pasteurisation" that allowed milk to be sterilized by heating it at very high temperatures for a short duration before packing and delivery.

❋ *Pasteurisation of milk*

EPIDEMICS AND PANDEMICS IN HISTORY

An epidemic is the rapid spread of an infectious disease to a larger than expected number of people in a given population, whereas a "pandemic" is any disease that spreads across a large region, different continents, or even across the world. There have been several pandemics in history, most of which were caused by bacteria and viruses and occasionally by others such as protozoa. Pandemics can cause disruption of society, economic loss and widespread hardships.

❋ *Black scabs and gangrene of hands and legs led to its name "black death"*

The Black Death

Among the different pandemics, the Black Death in Europe is the most well-known. It refers to a plague outbreak caused by the bacterial species Yersinia pestis. The reason why plague is known as "black death" is because it causes sores in the skin that develop into black scabs over time.

The bubonic plague pandemic of the 14th century, which caused swelling known as 'buboes" in the glands of the neck and armpits, is considered to have originated in Asia, spreading to Europe through rats transported across continents in merchant ships. Ports were major centres of human activity and the bacteria spread quickly from rat fleas that transmitted the bacteria from the rats to people. Between 1343 and 1356, the plague killed 75 to 200 million people in Europe, Africa and Asia.

❋ *Close-up of a rat flea*

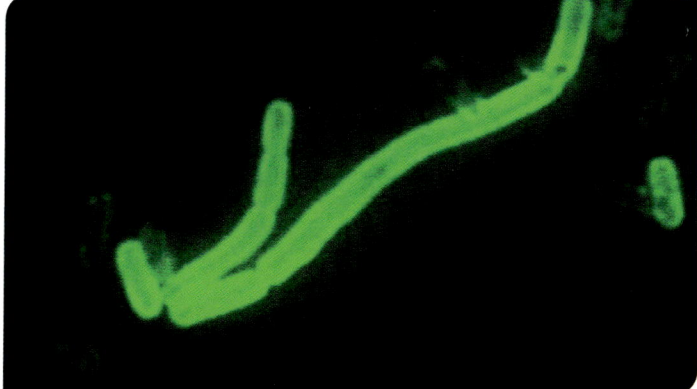

❋ *Bacteria Yersinia pestis that caused bubonic plague*

The Flu Pandemic of 1918

Influenza or flu caused by the influenza virus usually only affects elderly people, weak and ill patients or infants. However, the flu pandemic of the 20th century that lasted from 1918 to 1920 was so potent that even healthy, young people succumbed to the disease. In such a short span, it killed nearly 20 to 50 million people.

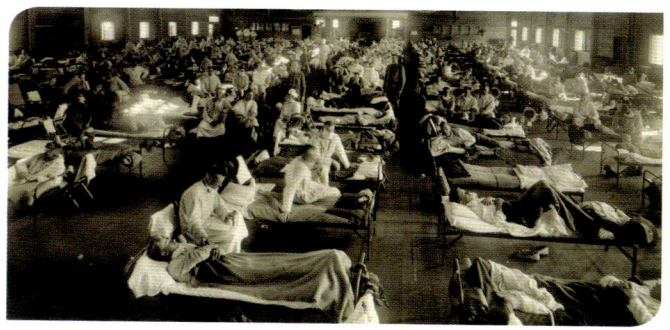

❋ *A temporary hospital ward to tackle the flu pandemic of 1918*

Malaria and the Roman Empire

Today, malaria is virtually non-existent in Europe and North America. However, in Africa, malaria still kills more than 2 million people every year. In ancient times, malaria was a deadly disease that affected populations across Europe. Mosquitoes and larvae were spread through cargo ships to Rome and affected people in the fifth century AD. The disease caused by the Plasmodium species was a contributing factor to the decline of the Roman Empire by killing thousands of people.

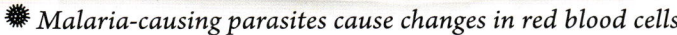
❋ *Malaria-causing parasites cause changes in red blood cells*

❋ *A painting showing a patient dying of cholera*

The Cholera Pandemic of 19th Century

There have been several cholera outbreaks in history, though the cholera pandemic of the 19th century lasting from 1852 to 1860 is considered to have been the most deadly. It originated in the Ganges river delta in India and spread across Asia, Europe, Africa and North America. Contaminated water was finally identified as the cause of the disease caused by the bacterial species Vibrio cholerae. About a million people died from the disease.

Even though cholera can easily be cured today through antibiotics and dehydration therapy, people did not have that luxury in the 19th century. Untreated, a major population of those infected with cholera succumbed to severe diarrhea, vomiting, and cramps which later resulted in fatal dehydration and septic shock. There have been several cholera outbreaks before and people travelling from one place to another spread the disease across a wide region stretching from Asia, Europe, and all the way to America.

Fact File
At the time of Black Death in Europe, people wore masks because they thought the disease spread through dirty air, not rats!

Typhoid Mary

In 1869, an Irish woman, Mary Mallon, emigrated from Ireland to the USA and worked as a cook. As a healthy carrier of the typhoid-causing bacteria Salmonella typhii, she was responsible for spreading typhoid through contamination of food to several people and refused to be quarantined. She infected 122 people in total and was eventually referred to as "Typhoid Mary".

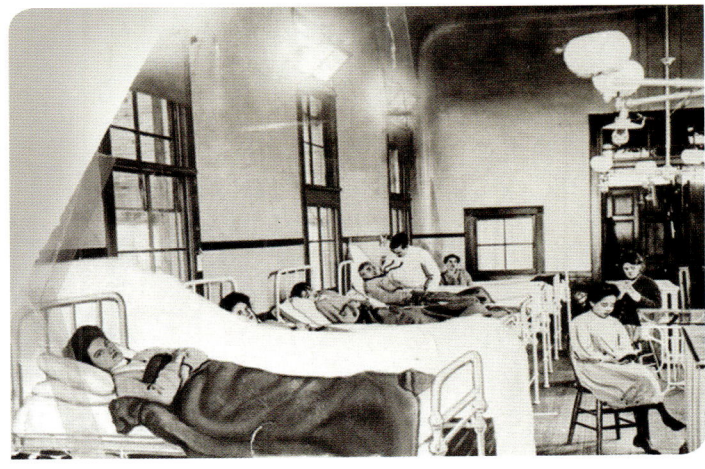
❋ *Typhoid Mary in the hospital*

STERILISATION AND DISINFECTION

Typically, people with different ailments and infections visit a hospital or healthcare centre to get treated. Sterilisation and disinfection are two primary methods for curbing infections in homes and in hospitals and clinics. Antiseptics and disinfectants eliminate harmful microbes and maintain a sanitized environment where spread of infection is effectively controlled.

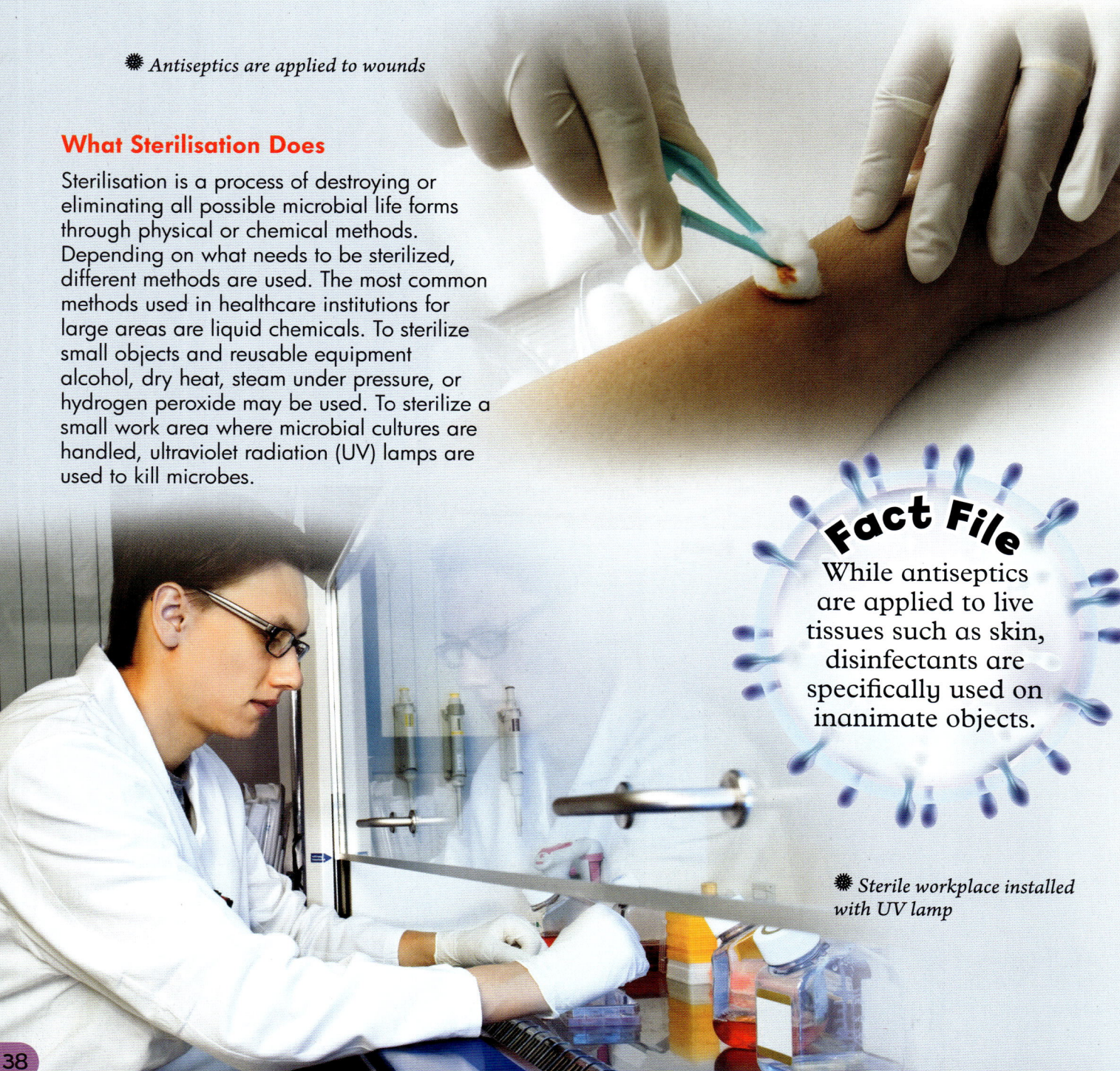

✺ Antiseptics are applied to wounds

What Sterilisation Does

Sterilisation is a process of destroying or eliminating all possible microbial life forms through physical or chemical methods. Depending on what needs to be sterilized, different methods are used. The most common methods used in healthcare institutions for large areas are liquid chemicals. To sterilize small objects and reusable equipment alcohol, dry heat, steam under pressure, or hydrogen peroxide may be used. To sterilize a small work area where microbial cultures are handled, ultraviolet radiation (UV) lamps are used to kill microbes.

Fact File

While antiseptics are applied to live tissues such as skin, disinfectants are specifically used on inanimate objects.

✺ Sterile workplace installed with UV lamp

✺ *The bubble boy, David Vetter, living inside a sterile bubble*

The Bubble Boy

For most of us, sterilisation and disinfection is necessary to keep away dangerous disease-causing microbes. Most times, our immune system is strong enough to fight microbes even if they manage to breach the lines of defense and enter into the body. But 1 in 100,000 people develop a severely compromised immune system that is about as bad as being completely "absent" due to a genetic disease called severe combined immunodeficiency (SCID).

The most famous person with SCID was "David the Bubble Boy" who, literally, lived inside a bubble soon after his birth and up to 12 years until he survived. The environment inside the confined bubble is completely sterilized. Even mild infections by any microbial species can lead to severe and recurrent infections. David was handled only through special plastic gloves attached to the chamber.

✺ *Powerful disinfectant can destroy spores*

Disinfection for Controlling Infections

This is a process by which all pathogens are eliminated through wet/liquid disinfectants. While this is an effective way to destroy most living microbial cells, spores are extremely resistant and may continue to survive. Certain bacteria exist in the form of spores that are highly resistant and able to survive even extreme high temperature and pressure. The efficiency of disinfection depends on the amount and type of microbes present in an area. While sterilisation can destroy spores, disinfection cannot unless the spores are exposed to the disinfectant for a few hours, at least. Thus, based on their efficiency, there are low-level and high-level disinfectants.

Depending on the type of microbe or parasite targeted, the germicides are referred to by different terms: bactericide, fungicide, sporicide, virucide, and tuberculocide.

ANTIBIOTICS

The word "antibiotic" means "against life". Antibiotics are designed to fight against microbial parasites that cause diseases in humans. There are different types of antibiotics designed to fight against specific parasites such as fungi, protozoa, bacteria or viruses. Broad-spectrum antibiotics are designed to fight against a wide range of microbes and are prescribed to treat multiple infections.

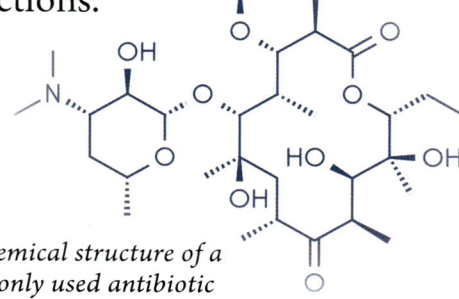

❋ *Chemical structure of a commonly used antibiotic*

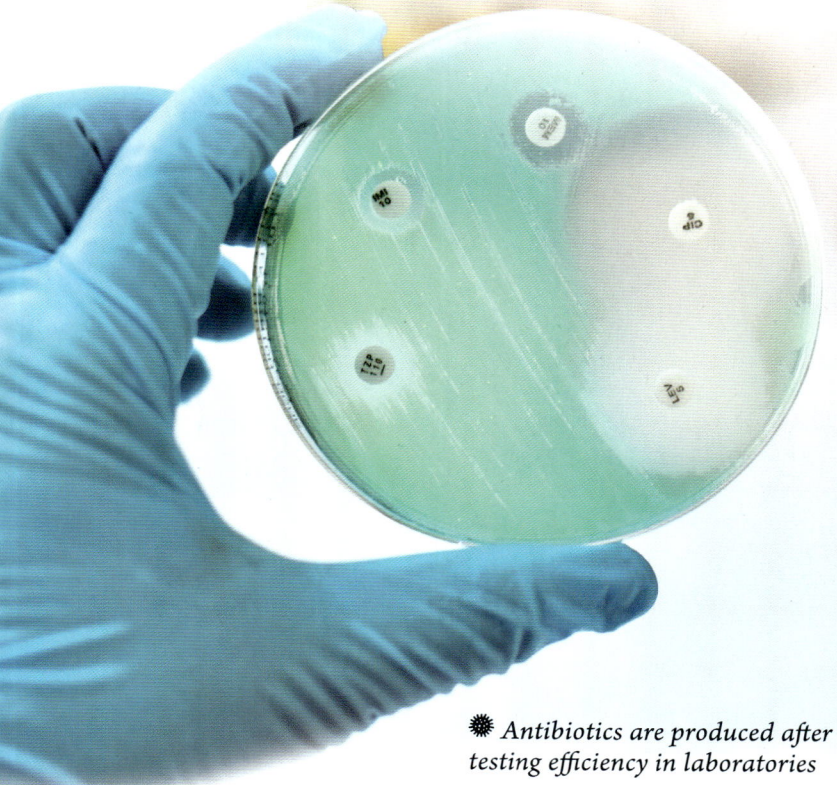

❋ *Antibiotics are produced after testing efficiency in laboratories*

Fact File
Fleming discovered penicillin by accident when he saw Staphylococcus bacteria species killed by a mold growing on the petri dish.

What are Antibiotics?

Antibiotics are chemical compounds that are designed to target specific bacterial infections, preventing their growth and multiplication. They do this in different ways – by stopping microorganisms from developing protective cell walls or dissolving a parasite's cell membrane or affecting its proteins. Antibiotics achieve the desired effect without causing any harm to human cells.

Discovery of Penicillin

The era of antibiotics began with the discovery of Penicillium strains and the development of the penicillin antibiotic. Alexander Fleming and his team spent nearly two decades developing penicillin and this was used widely on soldiers who were wounded during World War II and suffering from pneumonia and other infections. Today, there are thousands of antibiotics for treatment of a wide range of problems.

❋ *Penicillium sample presented by Alexander Fleming*

Antibiotics and Lifespan

There was a time when a diseases such as pneumonia or smallpox were deadly and without a cure in hand, people rarely recovered or survived after the disease. Diseases were particularly dangerous for babies and infants with lower immunity than healthy adults. The introduction and use of antibiotics has revolutionized medical treatment and increased the average lifespan of humans by nearly eight years! Even complex surgeries lead to excellent recovery thanks to different classes of antibiotic drugs administered to the patients to prevent any type of infection.

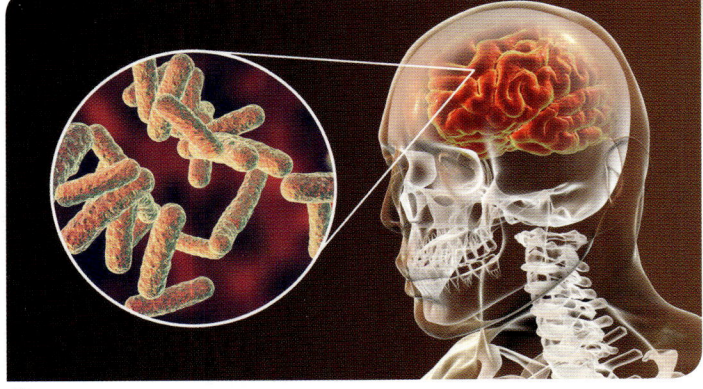

✸ *Antibiotics have helped increase average lifespan*

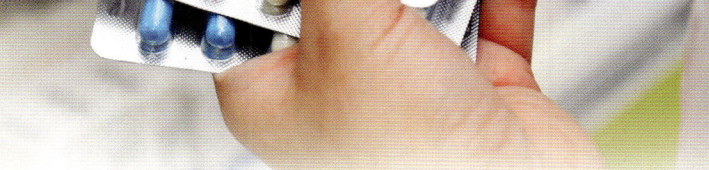

✸ *Bacteria can even infect the brain, causing meningitis*

The Downside of Using Antibiotics

Many physicians will examine your symptoms without writing you a prescription for antibiotics, especially if the effects of an infection are mild. This is to prevent reckless and excessive use of antibiotics for every ailment. By using antibiotics often, we destroy the natural, good microflora inside the body. Overuse of antibiotics causes bacteria to develop physical features that make them resistant to the antibiotic. This is, in fact, the leading cause of development of drug-resistant and increasingly potent bacteria.

Before Antibiotics

Different bacterial infections caused problems for children and adults alike before antibiotics were developed. People had only their own immunity to rely on to fight pathogens, and often the immune system had a tough time combatting resistant germs. Long before antibiotics were used, 90% of all children who developed bacterial meningitis died of the disease. Even those who survived developed serious lifelong symptoms such as deafness or mental retardation.

Back then, even a strep throat was sometimes fatal and even ear infections could spread to the brain. Diseases such as tuberculosis, pneumonia, whooping cough and diphtheria were incurable and often led to serious consequences.

✸ *Bacteria developing resistance to antibiotic*

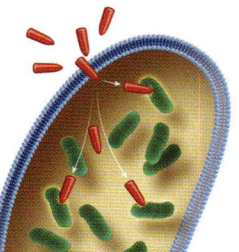
Antibiotics kill bacteria by blocking necessary enzymes

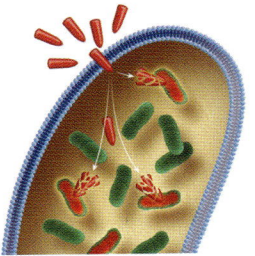
But bacteria employ sly mechanisms for evading attack. They spew out enzymes to slice apart the antibiotic

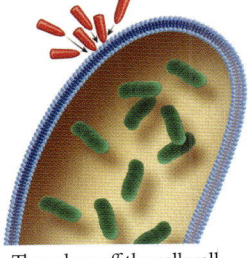
They close off the cell wall to prevent penetration

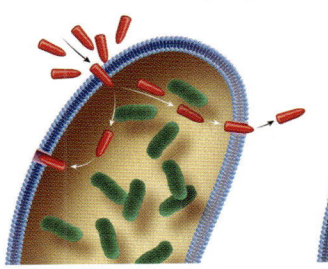
They pump out the antibiotic before it can kill

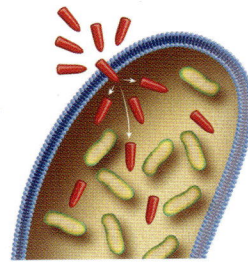
They change the target enzyme to disable the drug

VACCINATION

Vaccination is the process of introducing using dead or weakened pathogens into the body to elicit an immune response. This induced immunity works effectively the next time the body encounters the same pathogens, quickly and more efficiently. Today, new-borns and toddlers are given regular vaccinations to protect against a range of serious diseases.

The Story of Vaccination

Even though Edward Jenner, the British physician, is credited with the invention of the first vaccine, protection against smallpox was in practice much earlier. The Chinese used smallpox inoculation as early as 1000 CE. It was also a common practice in Turkey and Africa before it was an accepted form of treatment in Europe and America.

In 1776, Edward Jenner injected material from cowpox into the body to produce an immunity to smallpox – a deadly disease at that time. Over the next two centuries, vaccination has been further developed, modified and advanced to target and eradicate not only smallpox but also many other diseases.

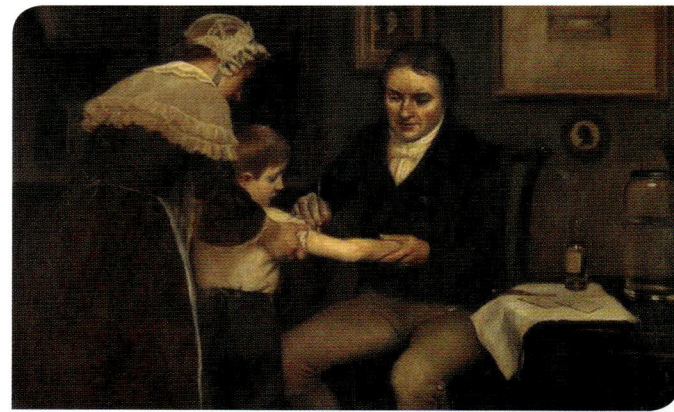
✺ *Edward Jenner developed the first modern vaccine*

✺ *Salk with his polio vaccine*

In 1885, Louis Pasteur developed a vaccine for rabies, another deadly disease. Following the research and developments implemented by these pathologists, several other vaccines and antitoxins against diseases such as cholera, typhoid, plague, tuberculosis, tetanus, and anthrax. Jonas Salk developed the Salk polio vaccine against the viral disease poliomyelitis.

✺ *Pasteur helped develop cures for many serious diseases*

Challenges in Developing Vaccines

One of the reasons why it was relatively easy to eradicate smallpox was because it was a disease that was only affecting, and being spread by, humans. Since there were no other intermediate animal hosts transmitting the infectious pathogens, global vaccination efforts paid off. However, for a disease such as yellow fever, which can be transmitted by monkeys, it is impossible to eradicate the disease even through vaccinating all humans, because there are monkeys in the wild that can still spread the disease. This is one of the main reasons why vaccination cannot eradicate all kinds of infectious diseases.

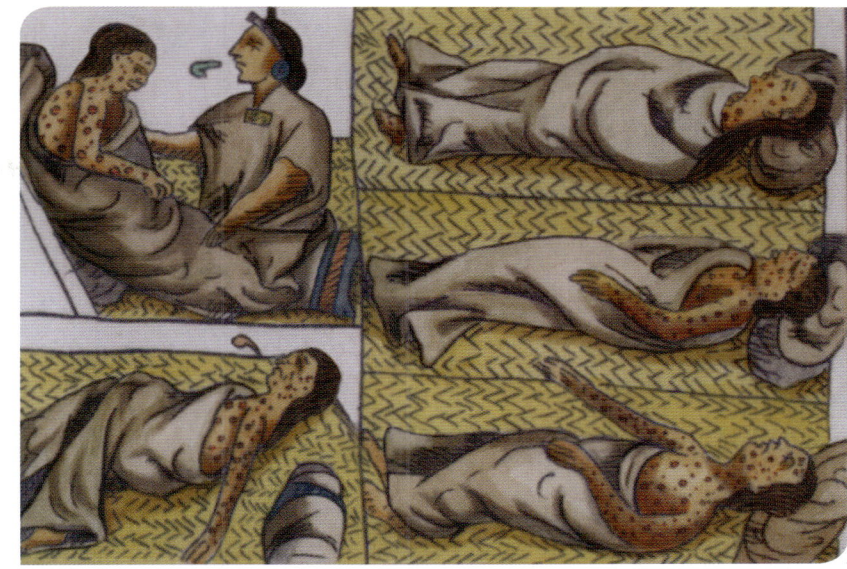
✺ *The effect of smallpox captured in a series of illustrations*

How Does a Vaccine Work?

A vaccine is a suspension of weakened (or dead) microbes or toxin that stimulates a strong immune response when injected into the body. When the B lymphocytes encounter it, they attack the cells and the lymphocytes turn into "memory B cells" that are sensitized to the foreign agent. Should the same microbes ever attack again, the immune response would be faster and more specific, thus preventing the disease. This is a way of developing artificial active immunity. Other vaccines provide passive immunity by providing antibodies already generated in some other animal or human donor. Not all vaccines are injected. Some are administered as oral drops or applied to the nasal passage.

Fact File
Smallpox, a dangerous viral disease, is the only human disease to be completely eradicated to date (2019), through vaccination.

✺ *A vaccine contains weakened or disintegrated pathogens*

BEST PRACTICES

Disease-causing microbes are present everywhere, ranging from the air we breathe to the soil we step on barefoot. Not all germs cause disease, and even among those that are capable of causing disease, not all are able to cause disease in people with healthy immune systems. Certain best practices ensure prevention of infection and limit the spread of diseases.

Mode of Infection

An infection usually occurs when microbes or parasites, responsible for a certain disease, spread from one person or vector (animal, bird or insect) to another. A simple task such as handling cat litter can result in parasite infection. A susceptible person has the right conditions for the parasites to gain access and multiply without being targeted by the immune system. Depending on the type of microbe or parasite involved, the symptoms of the disease may take a few hours to several days or even months to display any physical symptoms.

✸ *Even cat litter can carry harmful parasites*

Best Practices

Vaccines and a combination of antibiotics and other drugs and supplements are the best line of defence or treatment against diseases. Since bacteria, fungi, helminths and viruses are present in different sources, there are certain best practices that reduce the chance of getting infected.

1. Wash hands before eating: Wash your hands thoroughly before preparing food, eating, and after using the toilet.

Fact File
Sepsis is a life-threatening immune response to a severe infection. More than a million Americans are affected by it, every year.

✸ *Wash your hands thoroughly before handling food*

2. Get vaccinated per schedule: A family physician will provide a chart of all vaccines to be administered to a child from the time of birth up to a certain age.

3. Stay away from others when you're sick: When you detect symptoms of any contagious infection, it is best to stay at home until you recover. This way, there is a lower chance of the disease spreading to others.

4. Eat safe: Check vegetables, fruits and other food items in the refrigerator for signs of spoilage. Promptly discard old or rotting food and do not consume raw pork, shellfish or egg yolk as they have higher chances of carrying parasites.

❋ *Throw away old and spoilt food promptly*

❋ *Children should be vaccinated strictly per schedule*

5. Ensure hygiene in the house: It is important to use disinfectant liquids to clean the house so that all kinds of disease-causing germs are killed. It is also good practice to take a shower after visiting a hospital to prevent transmission of germs.

6. Avoid sharing personal items: Do not share items such as toothbrushes, combs, razors, clippers, kerchiefs, towels, or utensils. This is the best way to avoid transmitting infections.

❋ *Clean your house regularly with disinfectant*

INTRODUCTION TO CORONAVIRUS

Coronaviruses are a group of viruses that are capable of infecting birds and mammals. Like all viruses, they are capable of reproducing only inside suitable hosts. They were first discovered in the 1960s, both in chickens and in humans. These viruses typically infect the respiratory tract and lungs.

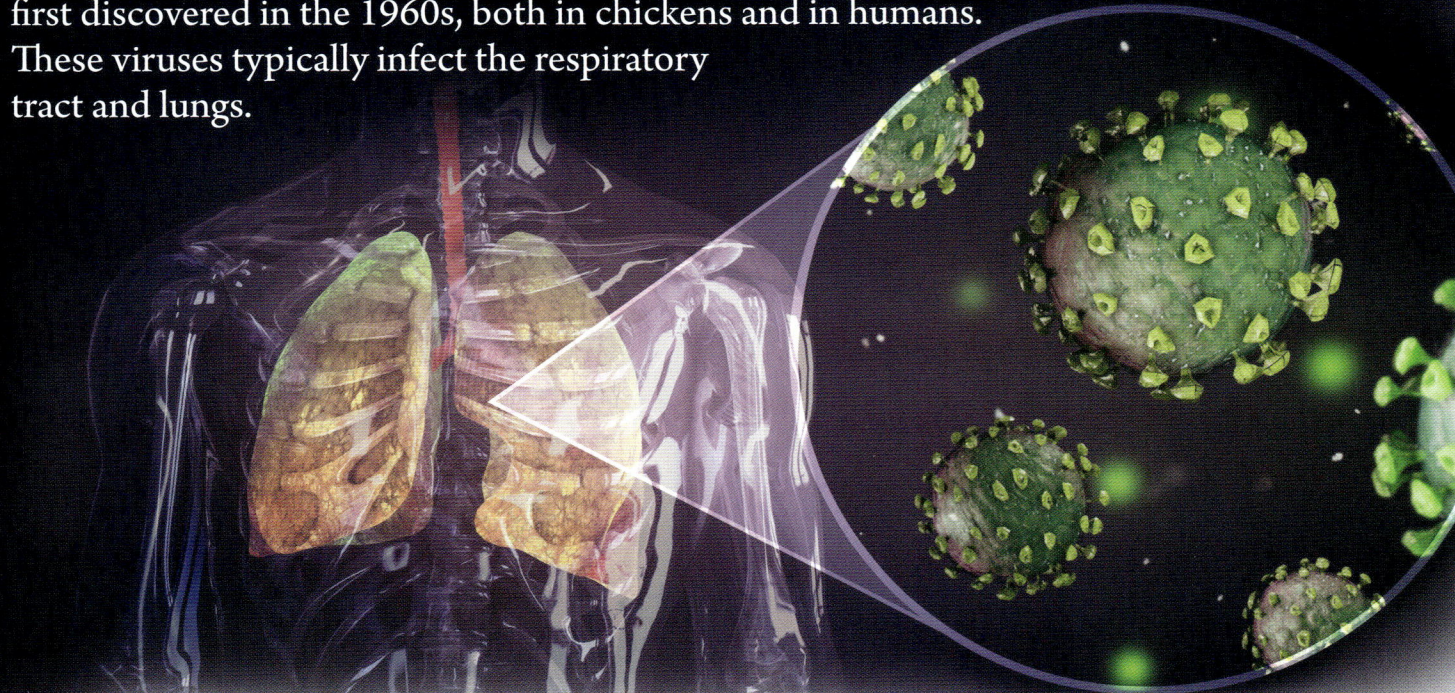

Virus: Tiny Infectious Agents

Viruses are unique on our planet for possessing the ability to thrive and reproduce only inside living beings. When they're outside a living host, they exist as "virions" – particles possessing genetic material in the form of DNA or RNA, a protein coat, and sometimes, a lipid envelope. Since they have all the components that other life forms possess but cannot thrive without other organisms, they are considered to be "organisms at the edge of life".

The shape of a virus can vary from an utterly simple helical structure to large, complex assemblies. However, most viruses are extremely microscopic and typically only about 1/100th the size of a bacterium. This makes it impossible to view them with typical optical microscopes except the ones that measure 700 – 1,000 nanometers.

Classification of viruses

Viruses of different forms, shapes, and sizes affect different organisms ranging from microbes like bacteria to mammals like humans.

Viruses are classified into groups commonly based on these characteristics:

- Type and nature of genetic material (DNA or RNA/ double strand or single strand)
- Presence or absence of lipid outer envelope
- Shape (icosahedral, filamentous, helical, complex)
- Size (small – 20 to 400 nanometers to large – 400 to 1,000 nanometers)
- Host (plant, bacteria, mammals)

✼ *Icosahedral virus (cowpea mosaic virus)*

Coronavirus

Coronaviruses comprise a family of enveloped viruses that have icosahedral (spherical) structure with spiky structures in the envelope. The name "coronavirus" is derived from the Greek word "corona" which refers to "wreath" or "crown". This is because, when viewed under an electron microscope - capable of high degree of magnification – they resemble the solar corona. It typically measures about 120 nanometers in diameter and possesses single stranded RNA as its genetic material.

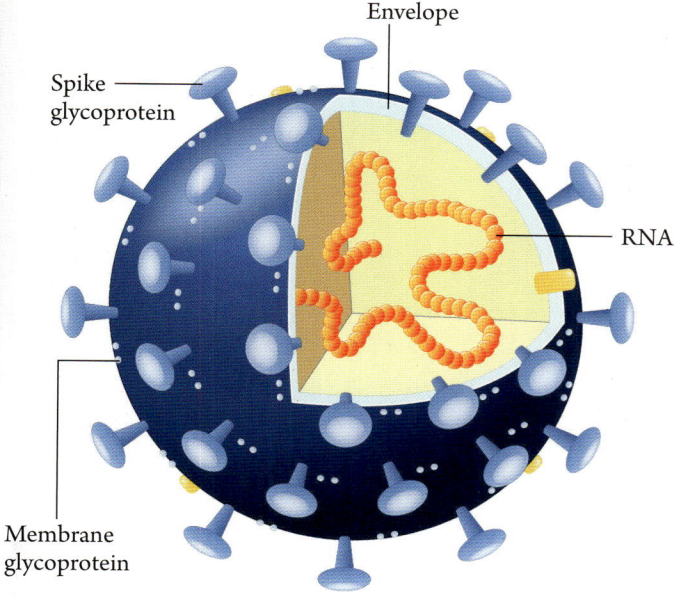

❋ *Cross-section of coronavirus*

❋ *The outer envelope of coronaviruses*

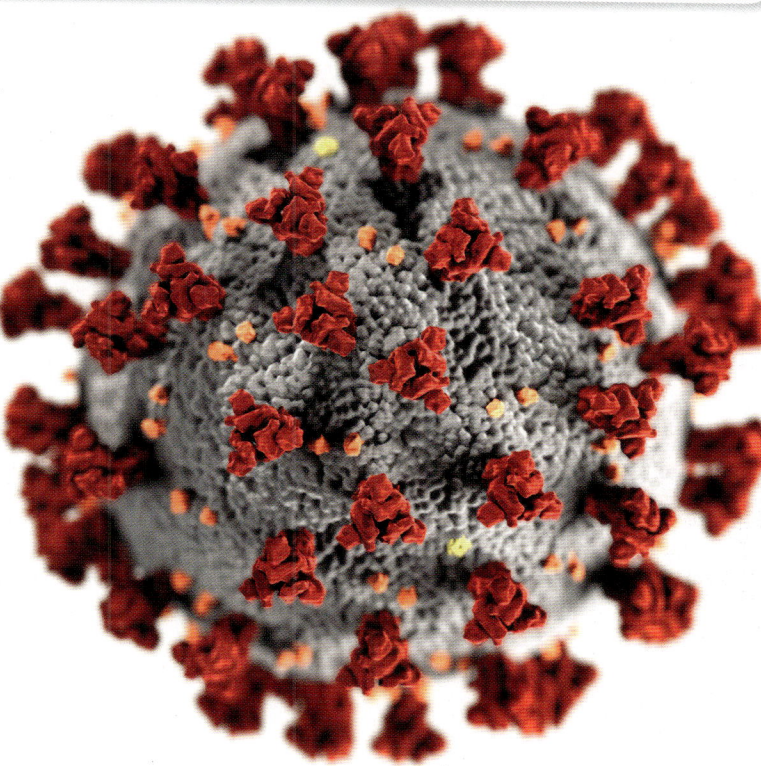

❋ *Coronavirus appearance*

What do coronaviruses do?

Coronaviruses infect birds and mammals and predominantly cause respiratory infections. The severity can range from mild common cold-like diseases to more dangerous respiratory diseases that can cause pneumonia and organ failure.

It's worth noting that as an enveloped virus, coronavirus is adaptable and can quickly change its outer structure to escape the host's immune system. On the other hand, the envelope also makes them more vulnerable to heat, detergents, and dryness, with limited period survival outside hosts.

Fact File
Coronaviruses are "zoonotic", meaning that they can transmit between animals and humans.

47

A BRIEF OVERVIEW OF PANDEMICS

Epidemics and pandemics are large-scale outbreaks of any disease, the former being confined over a geographic area while the latter has spread across one or more countries or even the whole world.

Worst pandemics in history

Infections and microorganisms have flourished along with the growth of human civilization. When humans live in close proximity to each other, microorganisms like bacteria, viruses, and protozoa spread. The overseas trading routes in the past and the connectivity today take the infection across to other parts of the world.

The plague, caused by a bacterial species called Yersinia pestis that spreads through rats, ravaged through Europe in 541 CE, killing millions. It returned in the Middle Ages, killing even more – about 400 million people died in just four years. It resurfaced several times over 300 years, killing nearly half the population of Europe.

Smallpox, caused by the variola virus, is currently eradicated across the world, but centuries ago it was a deadly disease that killed millions and left survivors with permanent scars. Smallpox is the first epidemic to have been cured by a vaccine, invented by British doctor Edward Jenner. The Spanish influenza pandemic of the 20th century is another outbreak of epic proportions.

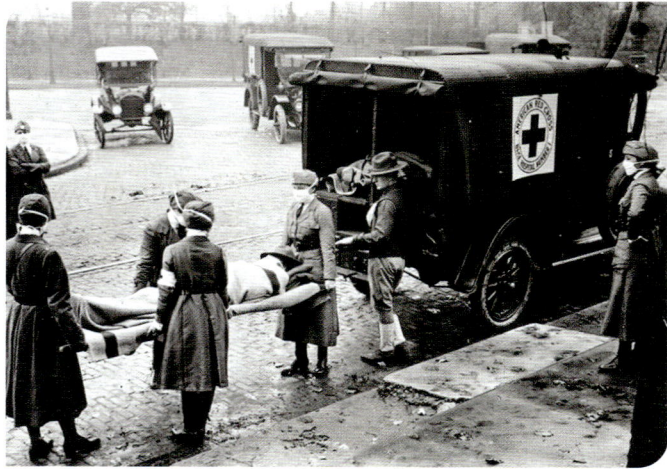
❋ *Spanish influenza pandemic (1918 – 20)*

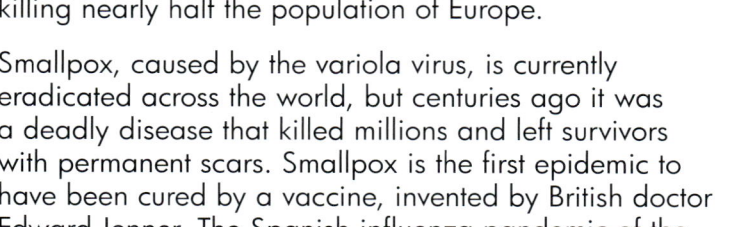
❋ *Painting depicting the great plague of 1700s*

SARS and MERS outbreak

SARS, or severe acute respiratory syndrome, affected thousands of people in 28 countries during the 2002–2003 epidemic. The SARS-CoV virus belongs to the coronavirus family and is thought to have transferred to humans from wild animals like civet cats or bats. SARS affects the respiratory system causing influenza-like symptoms. Of the 8000 people it affected during the epidemic, it killed nearly 800.

Another coronavirus strain MERS-CoV was responsible for MERS, or Middle East respiratory syndrome, with similar symptoms to SARS. MERS was also known as camel flu as people contracted it from touching sick camels infected with the virus.

The current pandemic of coronaviral infection is caused by SARS-CoV-2, also known as COVID-19. It causes symptoms similar to SARS and MERS, in that it results in a respiratory illness.

※ MERS virus viewed through electron microscope

※ SARS virus particles

WHO declares COVID-19 as a pandemic

The World Health Organization (WHO) was initially reluctant to declare the coronaviral infection that began in 2019 in Wuhan, China as a pandemic. However it rapidly spread to over 110 countries outside of China, reaching Europe quickly.

Even though the definition of "pandemic" can be a little fuzzy, it is given to any disease that spreads easily and rapidly from people to people in an efficient and sustained way. The spread of this coronaviral disease across the globe in just a few months explains its nature and severity.

Fact File
Bats are considered to be the natural hosts of the coronavirus, though it can also spread through other intermediary animals as well.

※ Map showing major European cities infected by the virus

※ WHO declares coronaviral infection a pandemic

FROM ORIGIN TO TRANSMISSION

The COVID-19 strain is more contagious than those that cause seasonal flu, swine flu, and Ebola but less contagious than SARS. Early projections indicate that 80 percent of coronaviral infection by this new strain result only in mild symptoms, while only 2 percent result in fatality.

Origin

As of March 2020, the Huanan Seafood Wholesale Market has not been declared as the origin point of the coronavirus pandemic, but it is officially recognized that two-thirds of the initial patients in Wuhan who had developed the symptoms of the disease were directly exposed to the market. The remaining one-third developed the disease even though they did not have any contact with the market.

The market dealt not only with seafood but also bush meat of exotic animals. The market was closed on January 1, 2020 in response to the initial outbreak. All other subsequent spread in other countries was through contact with infected family members, patients, and tourists.

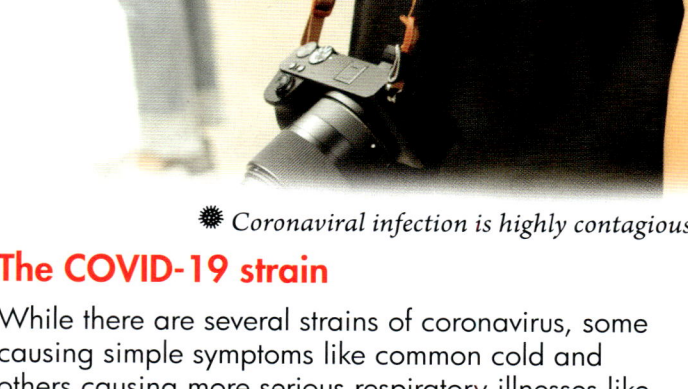

❋ *Coronaviral infection is highly contagious*

❋ *Pangolins may be intermediate hosts of viral transfer to humans*

The COVID-19 strain

While there are several strains of coronavirus, some causing simple symptoms like common cold and others causing more serious respiratory illnesses like SARS and MERs, COVID-19 is the name given to the coronavirus strain that caused viral infection and spread of disease in 2019.

COVID-19 vector

A vector refers to any living organism capable of carrying and spreading to other organisms a disease-causing agent. In the case of coronaviral disease, the infection is believed to have spread from bats to humans. Pangolins, or scaly anteaters, appear to be intermediary vectors between the transfer from bats to humans.

With the infection spreading among more and more humans, human beings are also important vectors for the spread of this disease.

Mode of transmission

COVID-19 spreads from an infected person through respiratory droplets. When the droplets land on a person's mouth, nose or hands, they can be inhaled into the lungs. The viruses can also be acquired without direct or close contact with a person through infected surfaces. The viruses can survive on different surfaces for different durations.

Fact File
The symptoms of coronaviral infection appear within 14 days of exposure to the virus.

● *Respiratory droplets during sneezing can spread the virus*

Signs and symptoms

The most common symptoms of a coronaviral infection are: fever, fatigue, and dry cough. Other less common symptoms include headache, dry cough, shortness of breath, muscle pain, chillness, nausea and vomiting. In very severe cases, high fever, pneumonia, and organ failure occur. In rare cases, conjunctivitis has also been reported in patients.

It is not easy to diagnose the disease simply through physical examination, especially when it is in the initial stage or milder form as it is very similar to common cold or seasonal flu. Because of this, doctors depend on laboratory tests to confirm the presence of the virus.

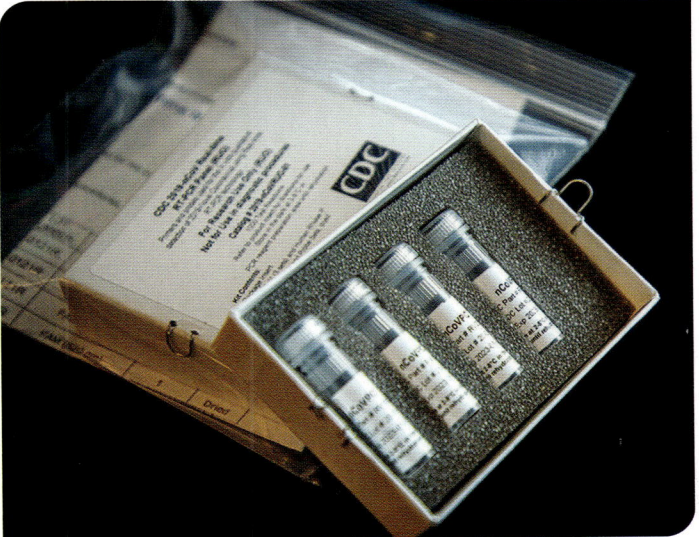

● *COVID-19 test kit*

 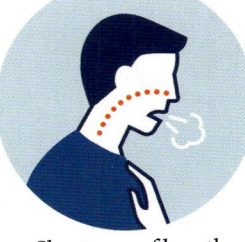  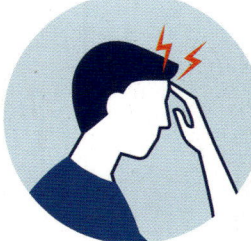

| Fever | Cough | Shortness of breath | Sore throat | Headache |

● *Symptoms of disease*

CORONAVIRUS OUTBREAK

The COVID-19 infection has spread to many countries, reaching around 160 as of March, 2020. However, not all countries were affected in the same way. The first few cases were reported in China. Soon, the outbreak intensified in Iran, Italy, Spain, the USA, South Korea, Japan, and to a lesser extent in several others.

✸ *Wuhan, the district where cases were first identified in China*

China

On December 10, the first among several infected patients was admitted to a hospital in Wuhan due to illness. Soon, many others followed, and patients were found to have an infection in their lungs that did not respond to regular drugs used for treating flu.

Doctors working in Wuhan Central Hospital began warning people about a SARS-like virus and by January 1, 2020, the seafood market that is thought to be responsible for the local infection, was closed. The WHO was also informed about the cases.

The scientists believed that the virus could not be transmitted from human to human, and no restrictions on travel or socializing were imposed. However, when the infection began to spread in China and gradually to other countries, travel bans and lockdown followed.

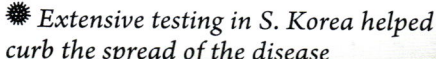
✸ *Extensive testing in S. Korea helped curb the spread of the disease*

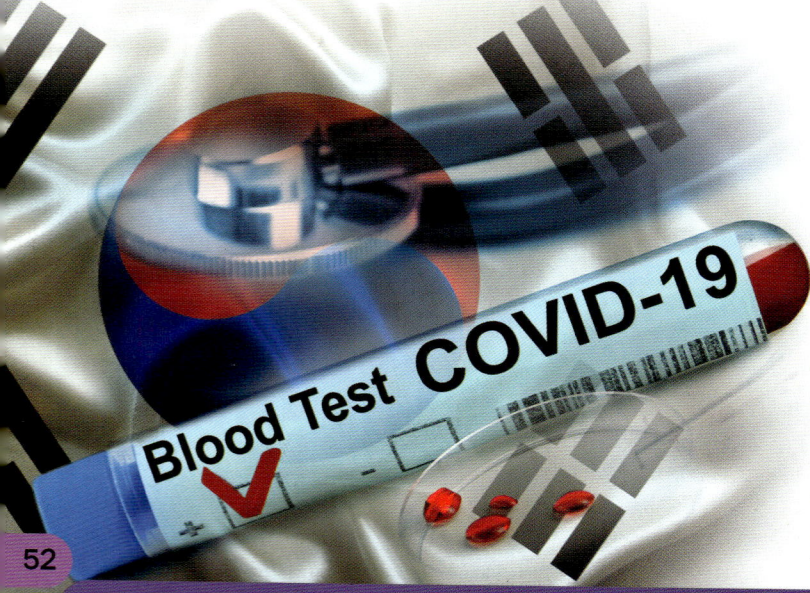

✸ *Italy was Europe's epicenter of COVID-19 infection*

Italy

It was on 31st January, 2020, that Italy recorded its first case, with the infection traced to two Chinese tourists who'd visited Rome and tested positive for the virus. Within two months of the first case, Italy had surpassed China's active cases and had a much higher number of casualties. A large-scale quarantine of over 50,000 people in the key affected areas was imposed to help the country deal with the outbreak.

South Korea

South Korea was another among the initially affected countries with thousands of cases but a lower mortality rate. The country was able to contain the spread of infection, largely due to extensive testing. Over 300,000 people were tested as of March, 2020 – around 5200 tests per million people – higher than virtually all other countries. The strict measures included releasing only people who tested negative twice and imposing heavy fines for quarantine violators.

Iran

The first known COVID-19 infections in Iran were recorded on February 19. The elderly couple who got infected were already suffering from other ailments and poor immune system. Like Italy, Iran also began to record high numbers of infections very rapidly, and within a month of the initial infection thousands had tested positive for the virus, with several cases proving fatal.

What makes Iran unique is the number of political officials and ministers who were infected. The health ministry, though it originally denied that Iran had many cases of infection, later began to take action to control the spread of infection.

✺ *People wearing protective masks in Iran*

✺ *Border checking for identifying travellers with COVID-19 infection*

USA

Even though the USA did not register many cases in the first few weeks after the outbreak in China, by March, the cases in the USA reached 50,000 with New York being considered as the epicenter in the country.

Fact File
With large numbers staying indoors, people played music and sang together from their balconies.

In Spain, number of confirmed cases per million inhabitants by province as of 26 March 2020:

- No data available
- Confirmed <50
- Confirmed 50–99
- Confirmed 100–249
- Confirmed 250–499
- Confirmed 500–999
- Confirmed 1,000–2,999
- Confirmed ≥3,000

✺ *Spain cases representative chart*

Other locations

Several European nations recorded cases, with Spain experiencing a sudden and alarming rise in the number of infections and casualties. The UK, Germany, France, and many other locations also recorded thousands of cases.

OUTLOOK AND AFTERMATH

The data collected across the globe provides valuable information and a basic outlook about the disease spread, control, and measures to combat it. It also helps countries struggling with curbing the spread learn lessons from other countries that managed to bring the situation under control.

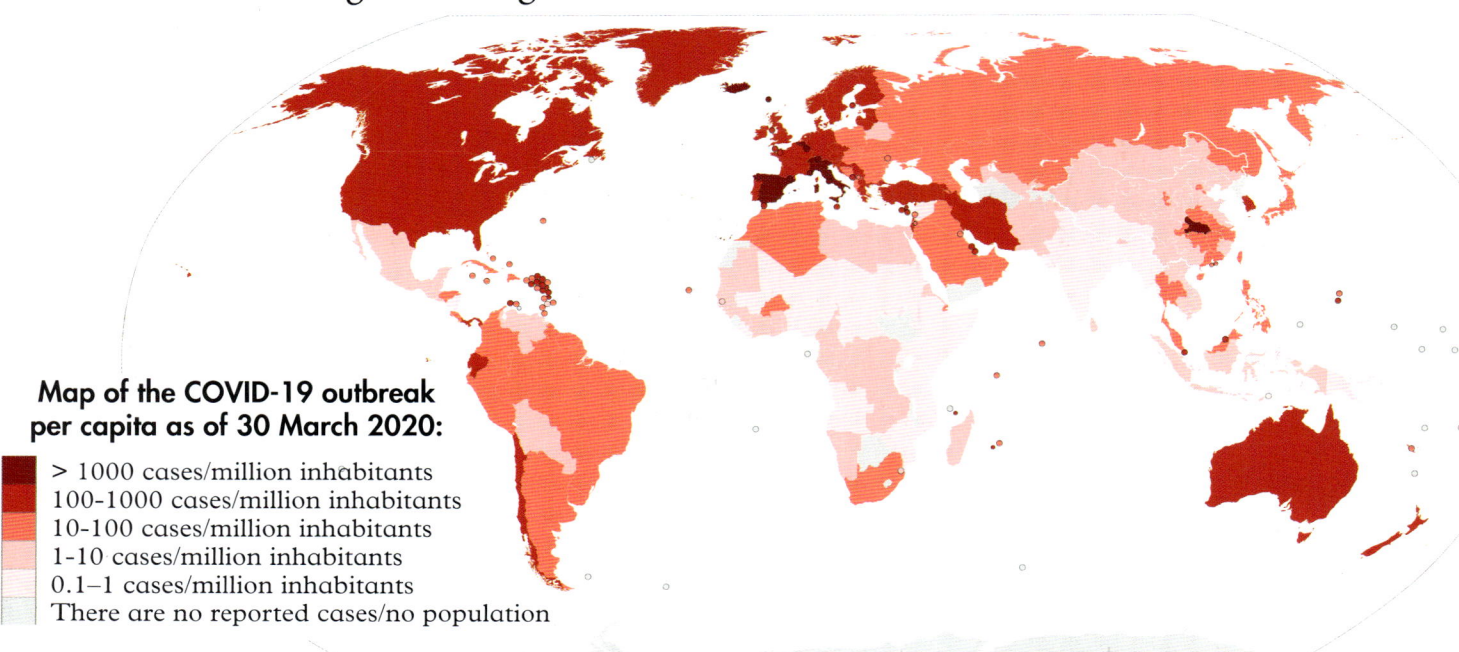

❋ Sample world data on coronaviral infection

Statistical report

Ever since the outbreak, countries have been meticulously collecting data on cases in different states, counties, and districts. This data offers valuable information about the disease trend and plans of action. The countries with the most cases or casualties vary every day and are updated on a regular basis to reflect the rise or fall in cases over time. A sudden spike in cases in a country can help the government figure out the cause and take the necessary measures to control the spread.

The data also provides vital information about the target population. For instance, no cases of viral infection casualties were recorded in children under the age of 10. Similarly, those people who already had existing problems with their lungs, heart disease, diabetes, or hypertension succumbed to the disease more easily. Another trend captured from the cases across the countries is the higher percentage of men infected by the virus than women, though there is no clear reason for it.

❋ Flu symptoms appear much earlier than coronaviral infection

What makes collecting data about the spread of the infection particularly challenging is its long incubation period which can be anything from 0 to 24 days. In comparison, the seasonal flu has an incubation period of 1–4 days. As a result, many countries are forced to wait and see how the infection progresses over time to get a clear picture.

Disinfecting a metro car

Fact File
At its peak, over 3 billion people around the world were locked down in quarantine to control the spread of infection.

The most important thing in the aftermath of the coronaviral disease is for people to take personal hygiene, self-care, and care for the safety of others more seriously than ever before. More than ever before, it is important for all countries to learn a lesson from the pandemic, and to be more prepared in case of another such scenario occurring in the future.

Aftermath

After the coronaviral infection slows down considerably across the world, economies everywhere will still take months to recover and stabilize. Even as schools, colleges, workplaces, and public transports in different countries get ready to admit their employees again, they have to be thoroughly cleaned, disinfected, and equipped with sanitizers.

Even after a reduction on the spread of the disease, research institutes across the world will treat it as a real threat and continue working on drugs, treatments, and vaccines for eradication.

Hygiene habits to be taught from an early age

SAFETY AND PREVENTIVE MEASURES

COVID-19 is a new strain of coronavirus that was first identified in 2019. Producing a vaccine for the disease will probably take several months, and no antibiotics will work, either. So, for people who want to be free of the disease, preventive safety measures are the best option.

❋ *Safety gear for hospital and healthcare workers*

Need for safety

Even for those living in a country already recording several people testing positive for coronavirus, it is possible to stay safe by taking preventive measures. Similarly, those experiencing symptoms similar to a coronaviral infection can isolate themselves, thus not taking the chance and potentially preventing others from catching it.

❋ *Self-quarantine can check the spread of infection to others*

This is particularly necessary if there are elderly people at home. Since they have a weaker immune system, they are more susceptible to the disease. People who are already suffering from ailments like diabetes, heart conditions, or respiratory problems also need to exercise caution.

❋ *Elderly people need special attention*

Precautionary measures

People across the globe are encouraged to follow these steps to stay safe during the pandemic:

- Avoid contact with those who have tested positive for the virus and already exhibiting symptoms.
- Stay home and quarantine yourself for a few days if you are feeling sick. Seek medical attention if the symptoms don't improve with rest and hydration.
- When you cough or sneeze, use a tissue and discard it after use or if you don't have one handy, use the crook of your elbow.
- Use a hand sanitizer after touching surfaces in public places or on public transport.
- At home, use soap or hand wash to clean your hands thoroughly for at least 20 seconds before cooking or eating. Do this also after coughing, sneezing, or blowing your nose.
- Clean and disinfect your house with a suitable disinfectant every day. Clean kitchen surfaces, table tops, knobs, and handles as often as you can.

Wash hands with water and soap/sanitizer, at least 20 seconds

Avoid contact with sick people

Don't touch eyes, nose or mouth with unwashed hands

Stay at home

Avoid contact with animals and animal products

Cover your nose and mouth with tissue or elbow when sneezing

Don't eat raw food, thoroughly cook meat and eggs

Keep objects and surfaces clean

Wear a surgical mask

❋ Safety measures infographic

Hospital safety and quarantine

Since COVID-19 is so effective at spreading from person to person, health care personnel and patients in hospitals and clinics are at high risk. High-risk patients are isolated within the hospital premises while those exhibiting mild symptoms are sent home to quarantine themselves for about two weeks. Face masks, gloves, and other protective measures are necessary while treating patients.

❋ High-risk patients are isolated

Fact File
Wearing face masks is unnecessary unless you have the infection or are taking care of someone who is infected.

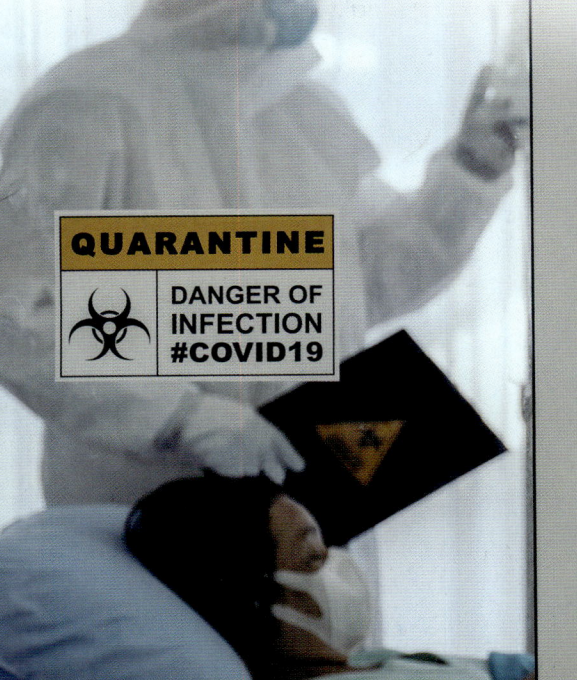

THE STEALTHY VIRUS AND REMEDIES

With COVID-19 infections causing infections across the world, healthcare and scientific research institutions have been trying to come up with a cure or vaccine to control and curb the disease. However, developing vaccines or medicines for any infection pose several challenges.

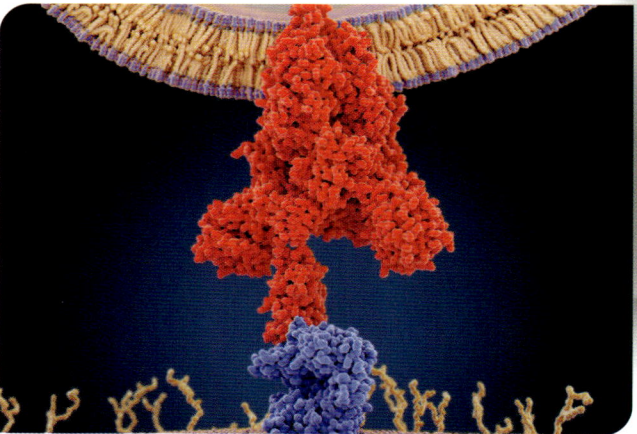

❋ *Coronavirus protein locking in with human protein to gain entry*

Stealthy viruses

Viral infections are difficult to treat because viruses are notoriously clever at evading the host's immune system. Also, viruses thrive and reproduce inside host cells. They do this by using proteins to gain entry into human cells and hijacking them, turning the cells into viral factories to make thousands of viral copies.

In the case of coronaviral disease, it is the lung cells that are most vulnerable because they possess more proteins that COVID-19 uses for gaining entry into cells. It is the death of lung cells that result in respiratory failure.

❋ *Mechanical ventilators are necessary in severe cases*

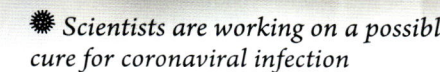

❋ *Scientists are working on a possible cure for coronaviral infection*

Current treatments

For most patients with mild symptoms, rest and fluids are recommended. For those with severe infections, the supportive care options in hospitals include supplying oxygen through mechanical ventilators.

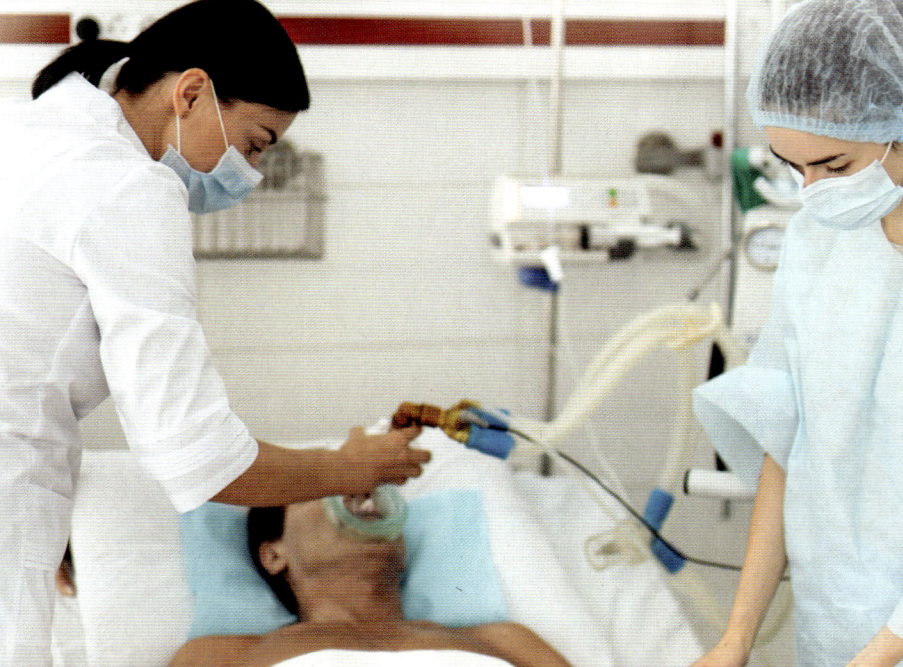

A medical research team

The options for fighting coronaviral disease

The usual way of fighting viral infections is through drugs that target viral proteins, preventing them from infecting cells. One of the drugs developed in clinical trials is remdesivir (originally designed for treating Ebola virus infection) that can target viral proteins. However, the problem with the long-term efficiency of this drug is that viruses constantly mutate and change over time, rendering any drug ineffective after a period of time.

Another more effective approach for a medicine against coronavirus is to design one that can prevent viral proteins from interacting with human cell proteins. This drug will not depend on tackling the virus itself, and thus have the potential to keep working on, irrespective of the viral mutations.

The third and easier way to find a drug for the disease is to scan through pre-tested list of thousands of approved drugs to see if there is a suitable candidate among them to treat the disease.

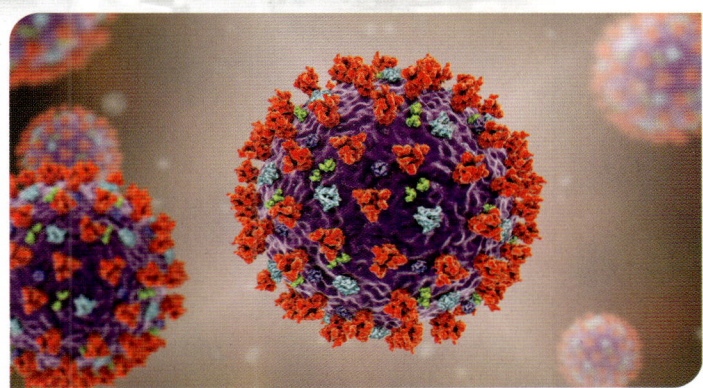

The viral coat proteins change through mutations

Clinical trials have been conducted in laboratories across the world on potential drugs and drug combinations for effectively controlling coronaviral disease. Some of the drugs being considered include remdesivir, chloroquine, ritonavir, lopinavir, and favilavir, and APN01.

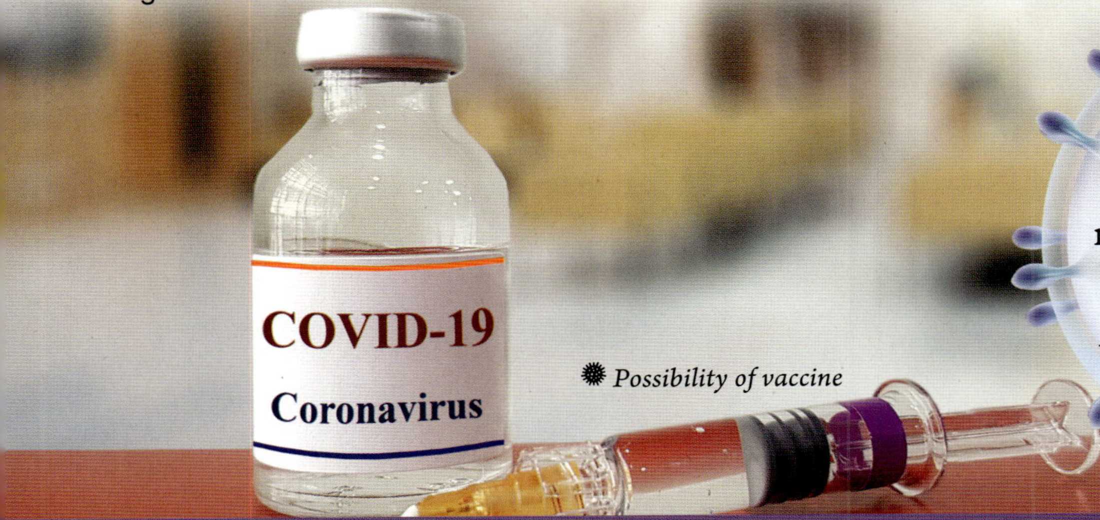

Possibility of vaccine

Fact File

Chloroquine, a drug used for treating malaria and arthritis, has been under investigation for targeting coronaviral infection.

GLOBAL IMPACT

Any major pandemic will take a toll on the global economy and also the lives of individuals across countries. The coronaviral infection of 2019-20 is no different. Some of the areas of impact include: the stock market, gold and oil prices, tourism, travel, business operations, and sales.

❋ Flights have been cancelled en masse and planes disinfected thoroughly

Travel and tourism

Among all industries, probably the one worst hit by the pandemic is the travel industry, especially airlines. With over 100 countries placing travel restrictions, airlines across the globe cut down most of their flight services. Needless to mention, all tourist destinations were locked down to prevent tourists from visiting or people gathering in any place. Countries that largely depend on tourism for their GDP have been majorly affected.

Stock market shifts

Due to panic among people around the world, the stock market experienced a major shift, with shares in different companies being sold or bought. Investors worry that stock exchanges have seen the biggest decline since 1987 and that the outbreak has the capability to destroy economic growth. Partially in an attempt to stabilize the economy, several central banks have slashed their interest rates.

❋ Stock market hit by coronaviral pandemic

Fact File
The tourism industry could take up to 10 months to recover after the outbreak is over.

Less customer spending

The virus scare and lockdown in many places left people buying fewer goods aside from essentials. The restaurants and food industry are majorly affected when people don't travel or visit places for leisure.

❋ *Many supermarkets exhibited empty shelves after people stocked up on essentials*

Slower work at factories and companies

With China handling about one-third of global manufacturing and as the largest exporter in the world, industrial production and exports slowed down considerably in the first couple of months in 2020 – by 13.5 percent – following the infection. The sale of cars alone dropped by nearly 92 percent in early February, and even in the days following the peak infection, people preferred ordering online to visiting showrooms.

❋ *Offices in China have been shut down after the spread of infection*

Hit on investments

Investors have been facing the full effect of the coronaviral infection on their investments, ranging from mutual funds to real estate to gold. Gold is always considered as one of the safest and most dependable investments, but even the price of gold started plummeting. The prices of oil have been the lowest since 2001. The Organization for Economic Cooperation and Development (OECD) predicts that the world's economy is at its slowest since the economic crisis that hit the globe in 2009.

❋ *Fall in gold prices*

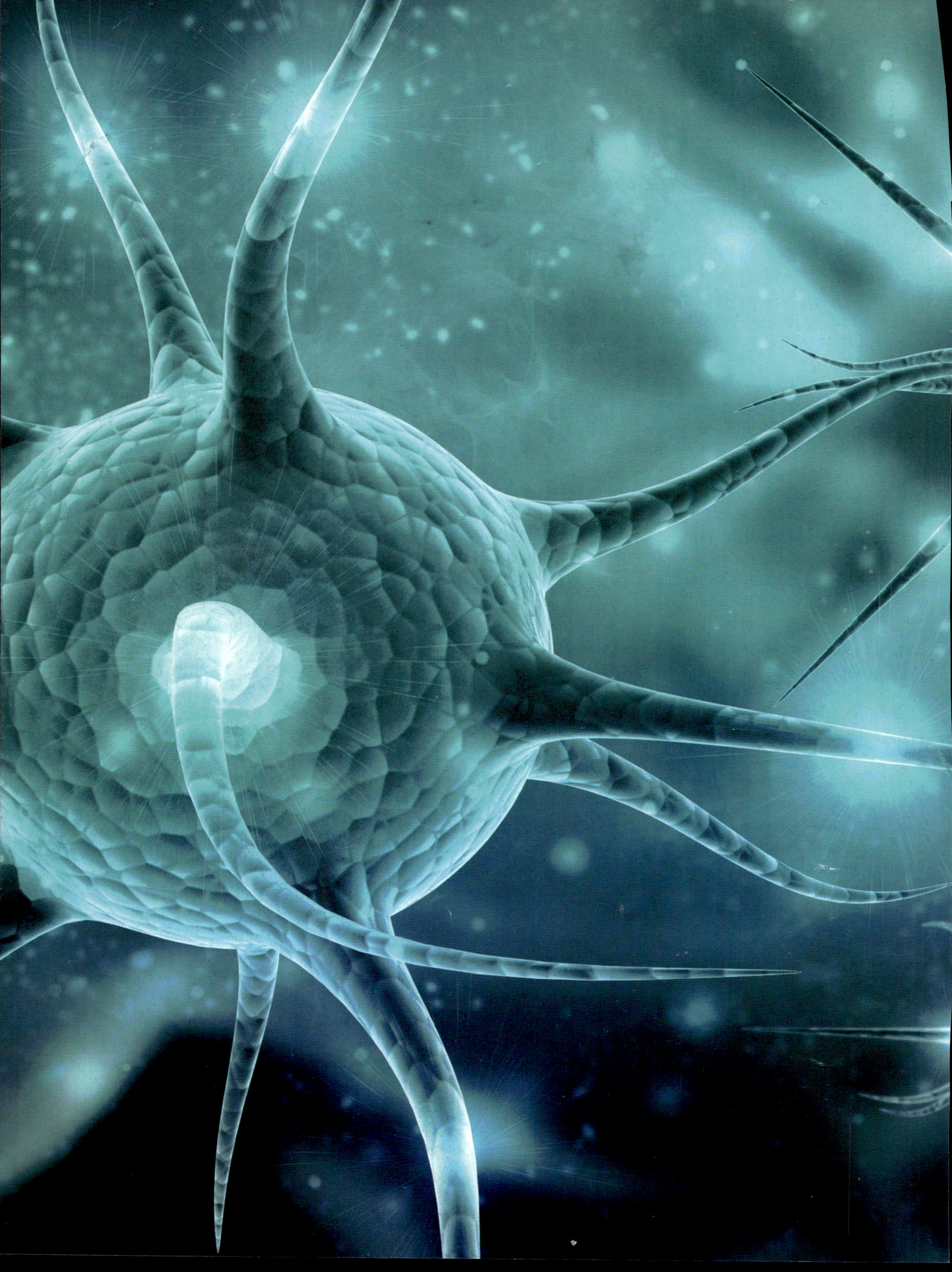

P40

P32

P67

Content Editor: Claire Bartlett
Editorial: Michelle O'Donnell and Leah Barton
Lead Designers: Leon Strachan and Craig McGregor

Published in the UK by DC Thomson & Co Ltd © DC Thomson & Co Ltd (2024). Registered office: DC Thomson & Co Ltd, Courier Buildings, 2 Albert Square, Dundee, Scotland, DD1 9QJ. Distributed by Frontline Ltd, Stuart House, St John's St, Peterborough, Cambridgeshire, PE1 5DD. Tel: +44 (0) 1733 555161 www.frontlinedistribution.co.uk.
EU Representative Office: DC Thomson & Co Ltd c/o Findmypast Ireland, RBK House, Irishtown, Athone, Co. Westmeath. N37 XP52. REPUBLIC OF IRELAND

EXPORT DISTRIBUTION (excluding AU and NZ) by:
Seymour Distribution Ltd, 2 East Poultry Avenue, London
EC1A 9PT. Tel: +44 (0) 20 7429 4000 www.seymour.co.uk

ENQUIRIES: ultimateseries@dcthomson.co.uk

4-5	**AMAZING ANIMALS OF AFRICA -** Lion Pride
6-9	Savanna
10	Cheetah
11	Meet The
12-13	All About
14	Hip-Hip
15	Gentle G
16-17	Learn A
18	Monkey Business
19	Super Survivors
20	Loveable Lemurs
21	Why Do Zebras Have Stripes?
22-23	Dazzling Zebras
24-26	The Science Of Giraffes
27-29	All About Rhinos
30-31	The Hero Herd
32-33	**AMAZING ANIMALS OF EUROPE -** Fascinating Foxes
34-35	Highland Tiger Uncovered
36-37	World Of Wolves
38	Night-Time Ninjas
39	Super Squirrel
40-41	**AMAZING ANIMALS OF THE FROZEN KINGDOMS -** Seal Of Approval
42-43	Winter Coats Of The Animal Kingdom
44-45	Beat The Chill
46	Frosty Facts
47-49	Penguins – Meet The Family
50-51	**AMAZING ANIMALS OF AUSTRALIA -** Cuddly Koalas
52-53	Marvellous Marsupials
54-55	Kickin' Kangaroos
56	10 Fun Facts About Quokkas
57	Sugar Glider Fact File
58	The Wonderful Wombat Of Oz
59	Dare You Meet... The Tasmanian Devil?
60-61	**AMAZING ANIMALS OF ASIA -** Gibbons
62	All About The Asiatic Bear
63	Golden Snub-Nosed Monkey
64-65	Magnificent Macaques
66	Orangutans
67-69	The Wild Side Of Giant Pandas
70-71	Clouded Leopards
72-73	Top Ten Tiger Facts
74	Wow! It Really Exists! Tarsier
75	Asia At Altitude
76-77	Red Panda
78-79	**AMAZING ANIMALS OF NORTH AND SOUTH AMERICA -** Bison By Numbers
80-81	Bear Necessities
82	All About Coyotes
83	Remarkable Raccoons
84	Let's Look At The Lynx
85	Cheeky Chipmunks
86-87	All You Need To Know About Ocelots
88	Cool Capybaras
89	Fast Facts About Slow Sloths
90-91	Jaguars Of The Jungle
92-93	The World's Loudest Monkey
94-95	Meet The Tapir
96-97	All About The Margay
98	Acrobatic Squirrel Monkeys

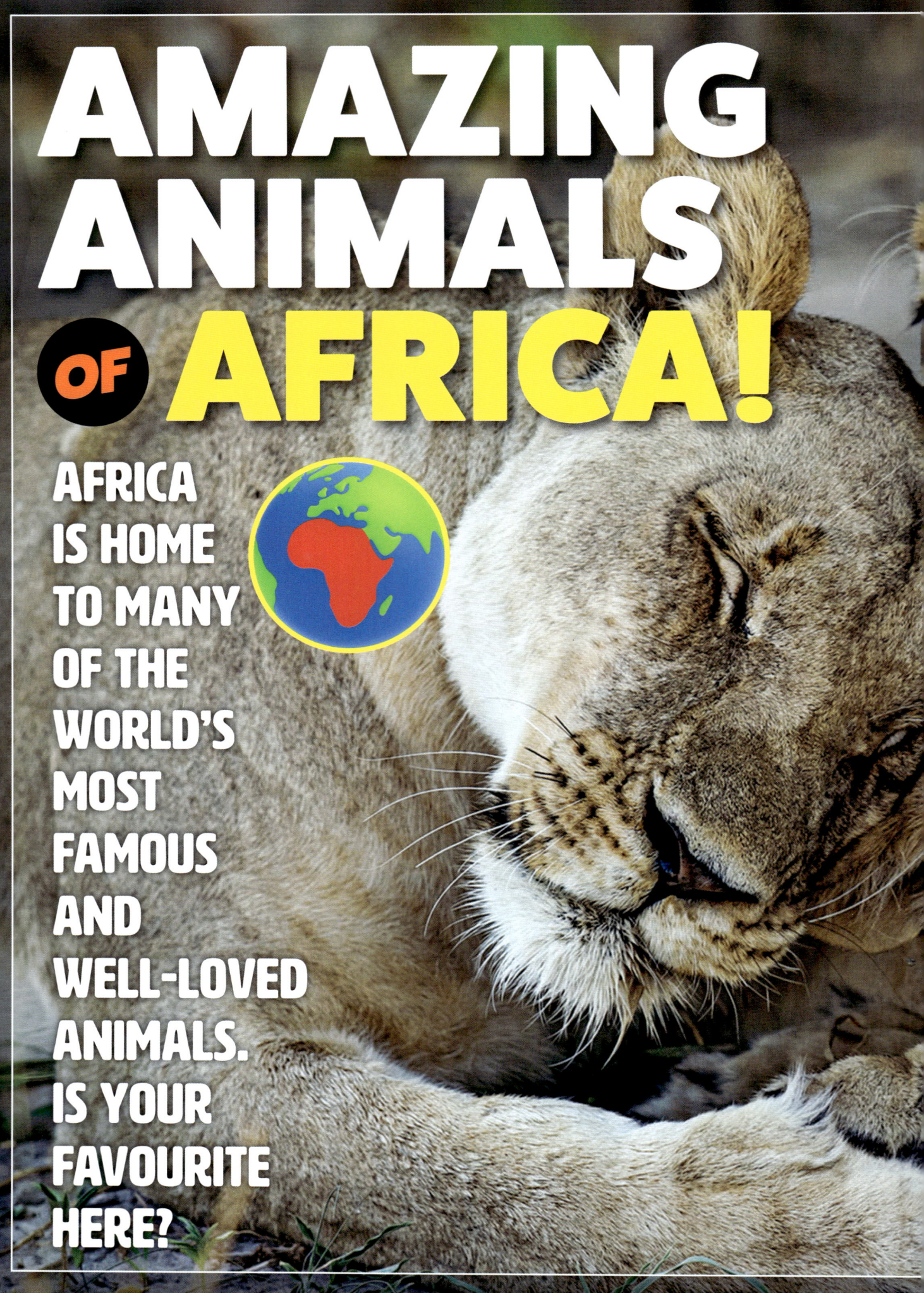

AMAZING ANIMALS OF AFRICA!

AFRICA IS HOME TO MANY OF THE WORLD'S MOST FAMOUS AND WELL-LOVED ANIMALS. IS YOUR FAVOURITE HERE?

LION PRIDE

LOVE AND PRIDE!
A pride is a group of lions usually made up of related females and cubs with one adult male lion. Lionesses raise their cubs together in one big group.

Lions live in very dry areas of Africa, and have to be creative by using plants to get a drink of water!

FUN FACT!
NEARLY ALL WILD LIONS LIVE IN AFRICA! ONE SMALL POPULATION OF ASIATIC LIONS CAN BE FOUND IN WESTERN INDIA.

DID YOU KNOW?
Male lions can weigh up to **190kg** (almost **30 stone**). This weight helps them bring down large prey when they hunt and to defend their prides.

ROAR-SOME!
LIONS ARE THE ONLY KNOWN CAT SPECIES WHO ROAR TOGETHER WITH EVEN YOUNG CUBS JOINING IN. THEIR ROARS CAN BE HEARD FROM **5 MILES** AWAY.

CUTE CUBS!
Young cubs are born with spots on their coats, which disappear as they grow.

SAVANNAH SAFARI

The Serengeti in Africa is home to hundreds of different animal species, but not all of them are large predators. There are also thousands of wildebeest, zebras, small antelopes, gazelles and more herbivores too. They co-exist in this ecosystem because they all tend to eat slightly different food.

SPOTTED HYENA
Best known for their unique laugh, these clever critters are dangerously good hunters! Real team players, they work in groups to take down large prey.

AFRICAN BUFFALO
Despite their scary horns, these animals are vegetarian. They can live in herds of a few hundred but have been known to gather in thousands. Herding together is one way to avoid predators as it's more difficult to pick off one member from a large group.

CHEETAH
The fastest mammal on land, this large cat can reach speeds of 60mph! They have large lungs, a strong heart, a flexible spine and long legs all to help them reach those speeds!

WHITE-BACKED VULTURE
Vultures feed on animals that have already died, making this scavenger a crucial part of the savannah's ecosystem – they're like a cleaning crew, collecting up flesh before it starts to spread harmful bacteria!

GIRAFFE
They can grow up to six metres tall and have feet the size of dinner plates! They also have long, purple-ish tongues which are used to grasp leaves and, just like a snowflake, no giraffe pattern is the same.

AFRICAN ELEPHANT
The largest land mammal, the African elephant reaches heights of over three metres and weighs up to six tonnes. Their trunk acts as an extra limb with 40,000 muscles in the trunk alone – they can even keep up to eight litres of water in it!

LION

The lion has perfectly adapted to this somewhat harsh habitat. Their fur blends in with its surroundings to make a brilliant camouflage for hunting.

Lions are sneaky hunters and hunt mainly at night as their eyesight is better than that of their prey. They also like to hunt in storms as the noise of the rain and wind makes it harder for their prey to see or hear them!

BLUE WILDEBEEST

The wildebeest, also known as gnus, are one of the largest antelopes. They migrate long distances and travel in groups for safety. Their name comes from the blue tinge in their coat.

ZEBRA

A group of zebras is known as a dazzle… and it's no wonder! Their white stripes ARE dazzling – when they move fast in a group it creates an optical illusion that confuses predators, known as a motion dazzle.

CARACAL

Recognised by its tufted ears and long legs, this wild cat is the heaviest and fastest of all the small cats!

MEERKAT

Expert diggers, meerkats avoid the heat of the savannah by making their home underground in complex burrows. They spend their days foraging for food like insects, with one meerkat acting as a lookout for predators!

CHEETAH CHAT!

Roar-some facts about this spotty big cat!

FAST FOOD
CHEETAHS PREY ON SMALL ANTELOPE AND HARES. THEY EVEN EAT BIRDS - WHEN THEY CAN CATCH THEM!

FAST FACT
They may be fast, but they can only maintain their top speed for a short time so sometimes give up on their hunt if they run out of energy!

FUN FACT!
Cheetah cubs will stay with their mothers until they're around 18 months old.

SPOT ON
SOMETIMES CHEETAHS ARE MISTAKEN FOR LEOPARDS, BUT CHEETAHS HAVE TWO DARK LINES RUNNING DOWN FROM THEIR EYES TO THEIR MOUTHS. THEY ARE FAMED FOR THEIR SPOTTED FUR AND BOAST AROUND 2,000 SPOTS, WITH EACH CHEETAH HAVING A UNIQUE PATTERN.

DID YOU KNOW?
ALTHOUGH CHEETAHS MAY NOT PRODUCE LOUD ROARS, THEY CAN STILL BE VERY VOCAL! CHEETAHS CAN YELP, CHIRP, GROWL AND HISS DEPENDING ON WHAT THEY ARE TRYING TO COMMUNICATE. CHEETAHS CAN ALSO PRODUCE A CONTINUOUS PURR JUST LIKE YOUR OWN PET CAT!

MEET THE MEERKATS

There's more to these desert-dwellers than you could ever imagine!

GIRL POWER!

Meerkats live in a matriarchal society, which means that a female is in charge of the group. This matriarch will lead the groups on foraging missions to find food, decide on where to sleep and also lead them into battle with any predators! When a dominant female dies, she is replaced by one of the oldest and biggest females.

TEAM PLAYERS!

Meerkats live in huge groups called mobs which can be as little as three or as big as 50. Everyone in the mob helps to gather food, look out for predators and take care of the babies. Being such social creatures, they love to groom each other and use their claws and teeth to brush and clean their fur.

FUN FACT! Meerkats are immune to venom! They can handle being bitten by some types of venomous snake!

THE MEERKATS THAT KEEP WATCH FOR PREDATORS FROM THE HIGHEST POSSIBLE PLACES, SUCH AS THE TOPS OF TERMITE MOUNDS, ARE CALLED SENTRIES.

MEERKATS ARE FOUND IN THE DESERTS OF SOUTHWESTERN AFRICA.

Everything you need to know about these cool creatures!

ALL ABOUT

FACT FILE

LOCATION:
Forests and grasslands of Africa and Asia

DIET:
Ants, termites and larvae

● **PANGOLINS ARE THE ONLY SPECIES OF MAMMAL COMPLETELY COVERED IN SCALES. TO PROTECT THEIR SOFT UNDERPARTS LIKE THEIR NECK AND STOMACH FROM PREDATORS, PANGOLINS CURL UP INTO A TIGHT BALL SO THAT ONLY THEIR SCALES ARE ON SHOW!**

THEY LIVE ALONE AND ONLY COME INTO CONTACT WITH OTHER PANGOLINS DURING THE MATING SEASON.

● There are eight species of pangolin currently roaming the Earth. Giant ground pangolin, black-bellied pangolin, white-bellied pangolin, and Temminck's pangolin can be found in Africa, and the Chinese pangolin, Indian pangolin, Philippine pangolin, and the Sunda pangolin can be found in Asia.

FUN FACT!

A pangolin's scales are made of keratin – the same material that can be found in our hair and fingernails!

Anteater

● This critter is nicknamed 'the scaly anteater' because of its looks and diet. Just like anteaters, pangolins rely on their sticky tongues for their meals, which are often longer than their own body!

PANGOLINS

FUN FACT! THE NAME PANGOLIN COMES FROM THE WORD 'PENGGULUNG'. THAT'S THE MALAY WORD FOR ROLLER!

HIP-HIP-HIPPO!

Their name means 'river horse' in Greek, let's discover why!

SCUBA SLUMBER

HIPPOS SLEEP UNDERWATER AND CAN HOLD THEIR BREATH FOR AROUND FIVE MINUTES AT A TIME. WHEN ASLEEP, THEIR BODIES KNOW EXACTLY WHEN TO RISE TO THE SURFACE FOR AIR WITHOUT EVEN WAKING UP!

A GROUP OF HIPPOS IS KNOWN AS A SCHOOL, SIEGE, POD OR BLOAT.

HORSING AROUND!

Despite their Greek name, hippos aren't related to horses at all. Their closest living relatives are thought to be pigs, whales and dolphins!

A hippo's skin is extremely sensitive to direct sunlight, which is why they stay in water for so long. When on land, they release a reddish-pink oily liquid that acts as a natural sunscreen!

FUN FACT!

THEY ARE THE THIRD LARGEST LIVING LAND MAMMAL, EVEN THOUGH THEY SPEND MOST OF THEIR LIVES IN THE WATER.

WATER BABIES!

They can spend as much as 16 hours a day in the water as this is the safest place for a hippo to keep away from predators like lions or hyenas. However, hippos can't actually swim! Instead, they glide through the water, pushing themselves off various objects including the riverbed.

GENTLE GIANTS!

Quit monkeying around and read these facts!

Gorillas live in small family groups of about ten gorillas. These groups are called troops.

Much like human fingerprints, gorillas each have a unique nose print!

A silverback gorilla can weigh up to 180kg — that's as heavy as a refrigerator!

Males aged between 8 and 12 are called blackbacks. At 12, a section of hair on their backs turns silver, giving them the name silverbacks.

Gorillas can eat all day! 85% of their diet is made up of leaves, shoots and stems but they add in the odd snail or ant.

COME DINE WITH ME-OW!

With their camouflaged fur, power, stealth, speed, sharp teeth and claws, leopards are excellent hunters. They will often use their strength to drag their prey into a tree to stop other predators pinching it! Leopards will eat almost anything they can catch including monkeys, deer and even young giraffes! However, leopards are one of the few big cats who are excellent swimmers and will also eat fish and crabs!

DID YOU KNOW? Leopards are the shortest of all the big cats!

LEARN ALL ABOUT LEOPARDS!

THESE FACTS WILL KNOCK YOUR SPOTS OFF!

CHATTY CAT!
TO COMMUNICATE WITH EACH OTHER, THEY USE A VARIETY OF DIFFERENT SOUNDS SUCH AS A ROAR, CHUFF, GROWL, PURR OR GRUNT. THE MAIN METHOD OF COMMUNICATION IS VIA SCENT. THEY WILL SPRAY THEIR WEE ON TREES AND THE GROUND TO LET OTHER LEOPARDS KNOW THEY ARE AROUND.

TREETOP TABBY!
Their tails are very long to help them balance when they are climbing trees. They spend a lot of the day resting in the branches of trees and are more active at night when they hunt.

SPOTTED!
LEOPARDS HAVE A VERY DISTINCTIVE COAT, BUT THEIR FUR ISN'T SPOTTY – THE PATTERN LOOKS MORE LIKE LITTLE ROSETTES. EVEN ON BLACK LEOPARDS, YOU CAN STILL SEE THE ROSETTES ON THEIR FUR.

CAT-LYMPICS!
They can run up to 38 miles per hour which is super-fast! They're also excellent at jumping and can leap 6 metres through the air – that's the same as three adults lying head to toe!

MONKEY BUSINESS!

Let's spend a day in the life of these cheeky chimps!

GOOD MORNING!
They spend at least seven hours a day feeding, mainly on fruits including bananas, pawpaw and figs. After a big breakfast, chimps become less active and tend to lounge about.

SOCIAL TIME
Chimpanzees live in social groups called troops. Within a troop, the dominant male is the leader and all the others treat him with great respect. When chimps haven't seen each other for a while, just like us, they'll greet each other by holding hands and even kissing!

GROOM FOR IMPROVEMENT
They spend much of the day grooming each other, removing dirt, burrs, dried skin and ticks using their fingers or lips! When they're not grooming, chimps are snacking on berries and leaves.

AFTERNOON
Later in the afternoon, chimpanzees have an intensive feeding session. This time they eat their usual fruit, but they also search for insects, eggs from birds' nests and even small mammals.

GOOD NIGHT!
When it's time for bed, chimps will make a nest using branches and vines high up in the trees, safe from predators. Then it's time to get some well-deserved sleep after their busy day!

SUPER SURVIVORS!

How do camels survive living in deserts which can reach mind-boggling high temperatures with very little water? Their hump has the answer!

GET THE HUMP!
Camels are known for being able to go weeks without drinking water, but they don't store it in their humps like people think. Their humps are fat reserves that get converted into the energy they need to survive when water and vegetation isn't available. They also act as a way of keeping them cool as all their fat is in one place rather than across their whole body.

DID YOU KNOW?
Different types of camels have different humps. Dromedary camels make up 94% of the world's camel population and only have one hump, while Bactrian camels have two.

FACE FACT!
They have very long eyelashes and closable nostrils to stop sand getting in them during a sandstorm.

TOE-RIFFIC!
Camels are equipped with wide feet with two toes. The large, round shape of their feet helps camels distribute their weight which stops them sinking into the sand.

FUN FACT!
If you ever see a camel with deflated or droopy humps, this is a sign it has gone without food recently. Once the camel is able to refuel, its humps will perk up again!

MADAGASCAR IS HOME TO AN ESTIMATED 112 SPECIES OF LEMUR. HERE'S THE LEMUR LOWDOWN!

LOVEABLE LEMURS!

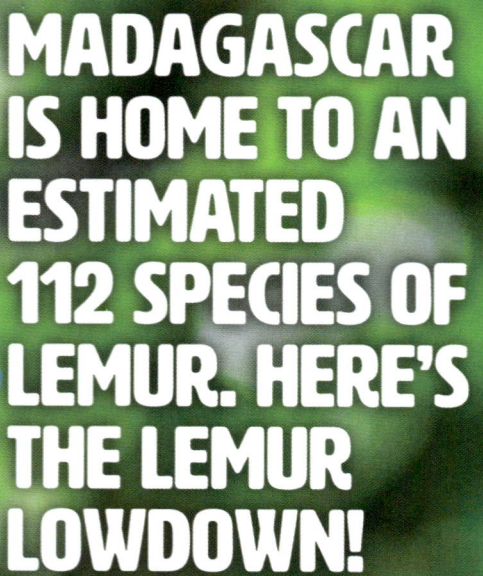

Madagascar is an island off the coast of Africa and is the only natural habitat for lemurs.

EYE DIDN'T KNOW THAT!
Other than humans, lemurs are one of the only primates that can have blue eyes. There is even a species of lemur called the blue-eyed lemur.

THAT STINKS!
Ring-tailed lemurs have a very unusual way of facing up to a rival! They have scent glands in their wrists and chests which produce a stinky odour they rub onto their tails and waft at each other until one is grossed out and leaves!

SHOW THEM WHO'S BOSS!
AT THE CENTRE OF ANY TROOP OF LEMURS IS A FEMALE. THEY SHOW EVERYONE WHO'S BOSS BY SNATCHING FOOD AWAY FROM THE MALES OR SHOVING THEM OUT OF THEIR COMFY SLEEPING SPOTS!

FUN FACT!
THE INDRI IS A VERY VOCAL LEMUR AND THEY COMMUNICATE BY SINGING TO EACH OTHER!

WHY
...DO ZEBRAS HAVE STRIPES?

ZEBRA FACT FILE
TYPE: MAMMAL
CONTINENT: AFRICA
DIET: HERBIVORE
HABITAT: GRASSLANDS

NOTHING IS BLACK AND WHITE
Except zebras! They are actually black with white stripes, not the other way around! Underneath that stripy fur, zebras have black skin too.

WHAT ARE THEY FOR?

Over the years there have been lots of different theories about why zebras have such vivid markings. Some scientists have thought they help zebras control their body temperature, while others have suggested that the stripes confuse predators by creating an optical illusion when zebras are moving in a herd.

HOW DO THEY WORK?
Another theory suggests that the stripes are to help protect zebras from being bitten by flies that might carry harmful diseases. The contrast between the black and white stripes makes it harder for flies to find a good spot to land on zebras. Researchers tested this theory by dressing regular horses in zebra-patterned jackets. They found that flies were more likely to land on horses without jackets than those wearing stripy coats.

DID YOU KNOW?
There are three different species of zebra – plains, Grévys (Greh-vees) and mountain zebra!

MEET THE SAVANNAH'S MOST FAMOUS STRIPES...
DAZZLING ZEBRAS!

ZEBRAS CAN SLEEP STANDING UP BY LOCKING THEIR KNEE JOINTS!

No two zebras have the same stripes! Each individual's pattern is unique, just like our fingerprints.

DO ZEBRAS HAVE RELATIVES?

- They sure do! Horses and donkeys are the zebra's closest relatives. Unlike their extended family, zebras have never been domesticated.

- Thousands of zebras will travel together in a super-herd to reach new feeding grounds. They can cover hundreds of miles in search of lush green grasses and drinking water.

DEADLY DEFENCES!

● Zebras are usually placid animals, but don't let that fool you... they pack a mean punch (well, kick!) when threatened. A stallion's powerful kick can even kill a rival!

HOME SWEET HOME

● All three species of zebra are native to Africa. They usually live in the grasslands and woodlands where they spend most of the day grazing on grass.

DID YOU KNOW? ZEBRAS ARE HERBIVORES.

BUILT FOR SPEED!

● An adult zebra can reach speeds of up to 45 miles per hour. Not quite fast enough to outrun a lion, but certainly speedy enough to get a good head start!

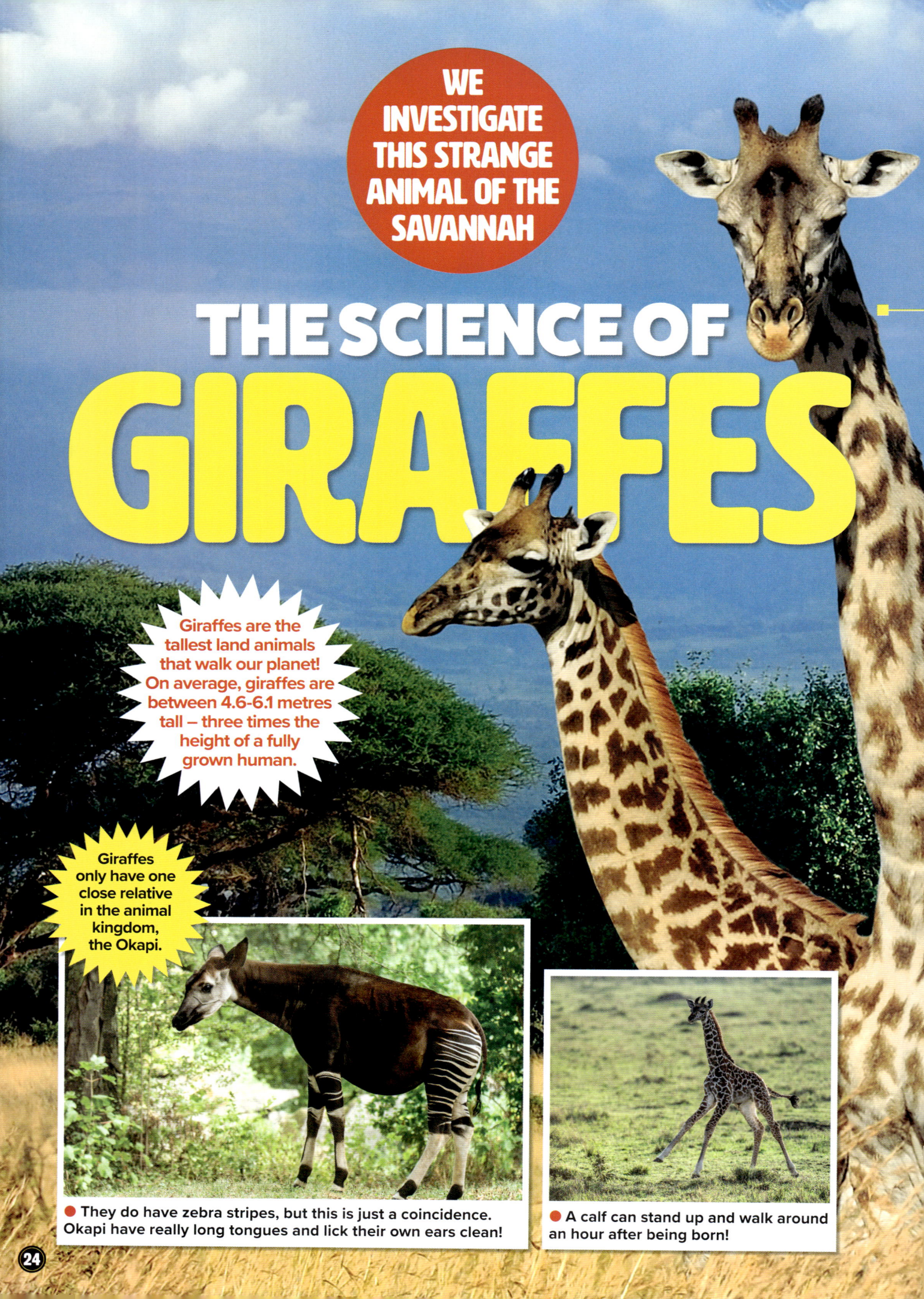

WE INVESTIGATE THIS STRANGE ANIMAL OF THE SAVANNAH

THE SCIENCE OF GIRAFFES

Giraffes are the tallest land animals that walk our planet! On average, giraffes are between 4.6-6.1 metres tall – three times the height of a fully grown human.

Giraffes only have one close relative in the animal kingdom, the Okapi.

- They do have zebra stripes, but this is just a coincidence. Okapi have really long tongues and lick their own ears clean!

- A calf can stand up and walk around an hour after being born!

THEY ONLY DRINK WATER ONCE EVERY FEW DAYS AND GET MOST OF THEIR HYDRATION FROM PLANTS.

They have really strong hearts to push blood around their incredibly long bodies. Their hearts can pump up to 170 beats per minute – that's almost three times a second.

● It's a good thing giraffes don't drink a lot because their necks can't reach the ground... so they do it like this.

LONG NECKS HELP THEM SPOT PREDATORS.

The spots are for camouflage in the dusty savannah. However, they also hide large blood vessels. These blood vessels help the giraffe remain warm as blood rushes to the spot and heats it up.

Giraffes love to stand up, they even sleep standing up. Amazingly, they only sleep between 20 minutes and two hours a day. Instead of sleeping for long periods, they have short power naps for a couple of minutes throughout the day.

THEY GIVE BIRTH STANDING UP SO, WHEN A CALF IS BORN, IT USUALLY FALLS AROUND 1.5 METRES STRAIGHT TO THE GROUND.

These legs help giraffes run up to 35mph when they're sprinting. That's faster than a car driving through a town! This speed comes in handy when they're escaping predators.

ALL ABOUT RHINOS!

We've got all the facts you need right here!

HOW MANY?

- There are five species of rhinoceros found on our planet. There are two types of African rhino (black and white) and three Asian rhinos – Sumatran, Javan and the greater one-horned rhino, which is also known as the Indian rhino.

WHAT DOES IT MEAN?

- The word 'rhinoceros' means 'nose horn' in Ancient Greek.

DID YOU KNOW?

A rhino's horn is made out of the same material as our fingernails!

FUN FACT!

A group of rhinos is known as a crash!

WHITE RHINO

Most of these amazing creatures live in protected areas of Kenya, Namibia, Zimbabwe and South Africa.

FUN FACT!
White rhinos are the second largest land mammal.

DID YOU KNOW?
The horns of a white rhino can grow up to 7cm a year!

RHINO TALK
Not only do they communicate through growls, trumpet calls and sneezes, rhinos also send messages to one another through their poo and wee – clever placement is used to let others know they're in the area.

FUN FACT!
DESPITE BEING SO LARGE, RHINOS CAN RUN UP TO 25 MILES PER HOUR!

SPOT THE DIFFERENCE!
White rhinos have a square lip whereas the black rhino has a hooked lip.

SMALLEST RHINO

Even though the Sumatran rhino is the world's smallest species of rhino, they can still weigh as much as 600kg!

LARGEST RHINO In comparison, white rhinos can weigh a whopping 3,500kg!

MUD BATH!

Rhinos love to roll in mud. It gives them a protective coat that keeps them cool in the soaring African temperatures and also helps stop insects biting them.

THE HERO HERD

JUST LIKE US, ELEPHANTS CAN FEEL ALL SORTS OF EMOTIONS. FIND OUT HOW IT FEELS TO BE AN ELEPHANT!

HAPPY-DERMS!

Elephants have been shown to display happiness and joy! They do this when playing around in the forest and while taking a bath, and also when meeting up with other members of their families. They are very vocal and will chat to the other members of their herd with trumpets and rumbles! Elephant herds are matriarchal — this means they're led by their biggest and oldest female, like the herd's mother.

DID YOU KNOW?
THE AFRICAN ELEPHANT CAN LIVE UP TO 70 YEARS IN THE WILD!

WHOLE HERD OF LOVE!

The bonds between members of an elephant's herd are extremely strong. They display love for each other by touching trunks and trumpeting happily.

DID YOU KNOW?
Elephants offer comfort by putting their trunks into each others mouths!

FUN FACT!
ELEPHANTS CAN RECOGNISE THEMSELVES IN A MIRROR!

ANGRY-PHANTS!

Just as elephants can feel joy and love, they can feel anger and rage as well! An angry elephant is incredibly dangerous as they weigh so much and are very powerful.

PLAYTIME!

Just like little children, elephant calves love to play. They race around and mimic each other and any older elephants in the herd.

The whole of the elephant herd is involved in raising the calves. If a calf's mother has to go and feed, another elephant will babysit the youngster until she returns.

AMAZING ANIMALS OF EUROPE!

Europe is made up of 44 different countries each with their own amazing wildlife and habitats from forests to snowy mountain ranges.

FASCINATING FOXES!

DID YOU KNOW?
FOXES ARE MEMBERS OF THE DOG FAMILY, BUT UNLIKE DOGS THEY CAN RETRACT THEIR CLAWS LIKE CATS DO.

FOX ABOUT TOWN
Foxes live just about everywhere – in the countryside, cities, forests, mountains and even in the Arctic. Foxes who live in or around cities will eat rubbish that people leave out... or rats! However, in the wild they eat berries, insects, worms and small animals.

FUN FACT!
A fox's home is called a den which is usually a hole in the ground.

FOX FAMILY
A FEMALE FOX IS CALLED A **VIXEN**.

A MALE FOX IS CALLED A **TOD**.

A BABY FOX IS CALLED A **PUP**, **KIT** OR **CUB**.

HIGHLAND

Thousands of years ago, the UK was populated by wildcats like lynx and cave lions, but now only the Scottish wildcat remains.

LAST CAT STANDING

■ It's thought that the greatest threat to the wildcat population is their ability to breed with housecats. Although reproducing is often a means to keep a species alive, this could actually make the species go extinct as the domestic cats' DNA takes over.

FEROCIOUS FELINE

■ Wildcats can measure up to one metre long, but they're sometimes about the same size as a house cat. Don't let that fool you! The Scottish wildcat earned the nickname 'Highland Tiger' not just thanks to its stripey fur, but also its fierce nature!

PURR-FECT PREDATOR!

■ Excellent night vision and powerful jaws make this kitty a formidable predator. They generally chow down on small mammals and birds – but they've been known to take down a deer before.

TIGER UNCOVERED

LOOK POO'S TALKING

■ Scottish wildcats have an interesting way of chatting to one another... through their poo! They mark their territory with droppings and another wildcat is able to figure out the pooper's age and gender from the smell!

■ You might spot a wildcat eating long grass, this isn't just for a tasty treat! It's actually to keep themselves healthy. The grass helps them flush out food they can't digest, as well as ridding their body of nasty parasites!

SPOT THE CAT

■ Wildcats are most active at dawn and dusk and are rarely seen in the wild. They don't like being out in rain or snow – just like domestic cats! If you go looking for one, you're more likely to come across its tracks or poop!

CAN YOU TAIL THE DIFFERENCE?

■ Although they look very similar to a domestic cat you might have at home, wildcats have blunt, bushy tails with a more rounded tip. It also has black rings down the tail and a black tip. It's more muscly than domestic cats with longer legs which help when it's hunting for prey on the mountains of Scotland.

WORLD OF WOLVES

There are close to 40 subspecies of wolf found living around the world, including Europe! Countries like Italy, Poland, Germany, Croatia and Romania all boast wolf populations. Grey wolves, or Eurasian wolves, are most common in Europe.

EURASIAN WOLF

- The Eurasian wolf is the most common subspecies of grey wolf. Although they mainly survive on livestock and rubbish left behind by humans, they are known to hunt in packs, preying on red deer, moose and wild boar.

Wolves are related to domestic dogs but have longer bodies and legs. They live to a similar age — around 10 to 12 years.

Wolves in Europe are not thought to be dangerous to humans - they can actually be beneficial! They control the number of deer and wild boar which, in turn, helps other animals and plant species to thrive.

COUSINS OF THE GREY WOLF

Let's find out about some of the other wolves of the world.

ARABIAN WOLF ▶

- One of the smallest species of grey wolf, the rare Arabian wolf, lives in small pockets of Western Asia and Northeast Africa. They tend to live in groups to increase their chances of finding food and have adapted to survive in dry, desert terrain.

◀ HIMALAYAN WOLF

- Found living in the Himalayas and the Tibetan Plateau, these wolves are perfectly adapted to life in the high-altitude mountains. Very little is known about these animals, but they're believed to be an ancient wolf that evolved before the more common grey wolf that we know today.

ARCTIC WOLF ▶

- Also known as the polar or white wolf, the Arctic wolf gets called all of these names because of the colour of their fur... and, of course, where they live! Their survival relies on the teamwork of their pack – after all, they couldn't take down a fully-grown musk ox on their own.

NIGHT-TIME NINJAS

MEET EUROPE'S FAVOURITE WOODLAND BANDIT – THE EUROPEAN BADGER!

Badgers are nocturnal animals and rarely seen in the daytime. They hunt under the cover of darkness, seeking out juicy earthworms, snails, slugs, fruit – and even the occasional hedgehog if food is scarce.

- **An adult badger can eat over 200 worms in one night!**

- European badgers can be found throughout Europe, from Albania to the UK. There are thought to be around **300,000** badgers in Great Britain alone. They live for five to eight years and can grow up to a metre long, from nose to tail.

- **Badgers usually have one to five cubs in a litter. The cubs are born in January and February and will stay in the warmth and safety of the sett until early spring. Once the weather is warmer and the cubs are around 12 weeks old, they will venture outdoors and learn to forage for themselves – under the watchful eye of their mother!**

- The badger is an expert digger, thanks to its strong front paws. They have a keen sense of smell which helps them locate prey or pick up signals left by other badgers. Scent marking is very important to badgers. They have several scent glands that produce different odours to alert other badgers.

FUN FACT Badgers are sociable animals and often live in groups called clans.

NEVER APPROACH A WILD ANIMAL - ALWAYS ADMIRE FROM A DISTANCE!

BADGER SPOTTING

Badgers like to live in woodland and open country areas - so this is where you're most likely to find them. You can use your senses to help you track down these elusive creatures!

SEARCH FOR... THE ENTRANCE TO THE SETT!
The hole will be oval-shaped and there may be some wiry badger hairs stuck to the soil. There's often a pile of earth in front of the hole too, which is created when the badger digs out the sett.

LOOK FOR... TRACKS ON THE GROUND!
Look at the mud and soil around the badger sett to see if you can spot footprints. They are quite distinctive – five toes with claws at the end.

SNIFF FOR... THEIR SMELLY LOO!
Badgers dig shallow dung pits close to their sett, which the whole family will use to deposit their musky droppings. Very tidy, but also very stinky!

SUPER SQUIRREL

How well do you know these remarkable rodents?

- There are more than 200 species of squirrel around the world.

- The world's smallest species of squirrel is the African pygmy squirrel, measuring no more than 13cm long.

- These common garden critters use a range of calls, including 'quacking' noises and territorial barks.

- Squirrels can reach running speeds of up to 20 miles per hour!

- Squirrels can be categorised as belonging to one of three types – ground, tree or flying.

- A SQUIRREL'S FRONT TEETH CARRY ON GROWING THROUGHOUT ITS ENTIRE LIFE!

- A squirrel's nest is called a 'drey'. Slightly lighter than a football, their nests are compact, ball-like structures made of twigs, bark, leaves and grass.

- Indian giant squirrels are the biggest species of squirrel in the world, measuring up to one metre long!

AMAZING ANIMALS OF THE FROZEN KINGDOMS!

FROM POLE TO POLE THERE ARE LOTS OF ANIMALS WHO CAN SURVIVE THE COLDEST OF TEMPERATURES AND THE MOST EXTREME CONDITIONS.

WRAP UP WARM AS WE TAKE A LOOK AT SOME OF THESE COOL CREATURES!

SEAL OF APPROVAL!

THEIR SCIENTIFIC NAME (PAGOPHILUS GROENLANDICUS) MEANS 'ICE-LOVER FROM GREENLAND'.

FURRY CUTE!
When harp seals are born, they are covered in fluffy white fur. The white fur helps to camouflage them from predators against the snow of the Arctic. It also keeps them cosy as they are born without blubber.

FUN FACT!
As they grow older, they lose the fur and gain a thick layer of blubber. Adults are grey with black marks.

FAST FACT!
HARP SEALS CAN SWIM REALLY FAST AND DIVE DOWN AS FAR AS 300 METRES! THIS HELPS THEM CATCH THE FISH THEY EAT.

DID YOU KNOW?
Mother harp seals can pick their pup out of all the other babies from their scent!

Winter Coats of the Animal Kingdom

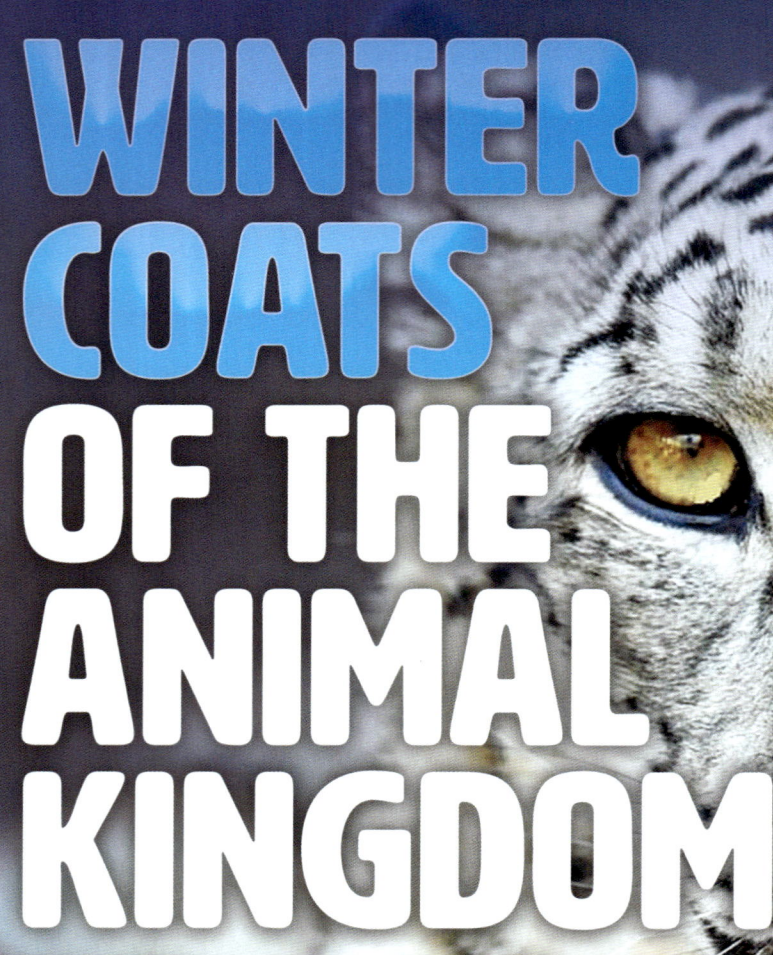

How much do you love your winter coat? There's no better feeling than wrapping up warm before setting foot outside when it's chilly. Animals are no different! Here are some awesome animals who use their natural woollies to keep warm.

FUN FACT!
MUSK OX FUR CAN REACH ALMOST 100CM IN LENGTH!

DID YOU KNOW?
Sea otters have the thickest fur of any animal found on the planet, containing as many as 165,000 hair follicles per square centimetre - we only have between 120 and 200!

ARCTIC FOX

- Although it may be hard to believe, Arctic foxes aren't white all year round. Instead, they grow their winter coat as the weather gets colder. Not only does it change colour – white helps the animal to blend into their new snowy surroundings – but it also grows through thicker compared to their brown summer coat.

SNOW LEOPARD

- Snow leopards' fur is much longer on their belly than anywhere else on their body, which helps keep them nice and toasty! They also have wide feet covered in fur, that act like snow boots!

ARCTIC HARE

- These white cuties are a little larger than your average rabbit, however, they are just as fast! Their striking white coats provide excellent camouflage in the winter.

MOUNTAIN GOAT

- Living high up in the mountains can only mean one thing – it's very, very chilly! That's why mountain goats have incredibly thick woollen undercoats, as well as hollow hairs that work to keep air trapped against the animal's body. All this helps to keep the cold and wet weather away from their bodies, allowing them to conserve warmth.

BEAT THE CHILL!

Here's how some other animals are perfectly designed to survive the chilliest of continents!

POLAR BEAR

WHITE COAT
This blends in with the ice and snow to camouflage from prey. Underneath, their skin is black, which helps to seal in heat!

FAT AND FUR
Thick layers of fat and fur keep the polar bear warm, insulating against the cold.

GREASY COAT
Helps to reduce heat loss by repelling water after swimming.

LARGE FEET
These furry feet balance the polar bear's weight and increases their grip on the slippery, often thin ice.

FOUND IN: THE ARCTIC

EMPEROR PENGUIN

SMALL BEAKS AND FLIPPERS
Emperor penguins have smaller beaks and flippers than other species of penguin to prevent heat loss.

FAT AND FEATHERS
Two layers of feathers and a thick layer of fat keeps them cosy.

FATTY FEET
Special fats on the feet stop them from freezing, and grip the ice.

HUDDLES
Chicks can't be on the ice too long, so will huddle with the colony for warmth to survive.

FOUND IN: THE ANTARCTIC

WALRUS

THICK BLUBBER
Blubber up to 10cm thick insulates against the cold and can be used as an energy source when food is scarce.

STRONG TUSKS
Tusks help the walrus to climb onto the ice, and are also used by males to fight for dominance.

BLOOD FLOW
Blood is directed away from the skin to the vital organs to keep them warm.

FOUND IN: THE ARCTIC

ARCTIC FOX

FLUFFY TAIL
When the fox sleeps, its fluffy tail acts like a warm blanket.

SMALL EARS AND MUZZLE
A smaller surface area helps the Arctic fox from losing too much heat.

COSY PAWS
Furry feet help the Arctic fox sneak up silently and stay warm.

FOUND IN: THE ARCTIC

FROSTY FACTS!

BEAR WITH US, AND WE'LL TELL YOU ABOUT THE POLAR BEAR!

- Their sense of smell is so good they can smell a seal under a metre of ice.

- Polar bears are classified as marine mammals rather than mammals as they depend on the icy ocean to provide them with food and a place to live.

- The Latin name for a polar bear is ursus maritimus which means 'sea bear'.

- POLAR BEARS ARE FOUND IN ALASKA, THE ARCTIC, CANADA, GREENLAND, RUSSIA AND NORWAY.

- Their paws are huge, measuring up to 30cm across. They have little bumps on the skin pads on the bottom of each paw which stops them slipping on the ice.

- A MALE POLAR BEAR CAN STAND UP TO THREE METRES TALL ON ITS HIND LEGS!

- A male polar bear can weigh as much as ten grown men and are the largest land carnivores in the world!

- THE LAYER OF BLUBBER THAT KEEPS POLAR BEARS WARM CAN BE UP TO 11CM THICK!

- WHEN A CUB IS BORN, IT'S ONLY ABOUT THE SIZE OF AN ADULT GUINEA PIG!

PENGUINS

MEET THE FAMILY

WHEN WE THINK OF PENGUINS, WE THINK OF COLD, ICE, SNOW AND THE ANTARCTIC... BUT DID YOU KNOW THAT OUT OF 18 SPECIES OF PENGUIN, ONLY EIGHT LIVE IN OR AROUND THE ANTARCTIC? LET'S MEET THEM ALL!

MACARONI PENGUIN

LOCATION: Antarctic Peninsula, islands in the Indian and Atlantic oceans, and islands close to Argentina and Chile
HEIGHT: Up to 71cm
WEIGHT: As much as 5.5kg

CHINSTRAP PENGUIN

LOCATION: Northern part of the Antarctic Peninsula as well as several Antarctic and Sub-Antarctic islands
HEIGHT: Between 71-76cm
WEIGHT: Up to 6kg

FUN FACT! They have the loudest call of any penguin!

DID YOU KNOW? Macaroni penguins can hold their breath for up to three minutes and dive down as far as 70 metres!

FUN FACT! Chinstrap penguins eat snow to cool themselves down when they start to feel too warm!

Macaroni penguins are the largest species of crested penguin (their 'crest' is the name for the yellow feathers on their heads).

DID YOU KNOW? They make their nests using pebbles!

EMPEROR PENGUIN

LOCATION: Antarctic
HEIGHT: Up to 130cm
WEIGHT: As much as 45kg

FUN FACT! THEY ARE THE TALLEST OF ALL THE PENGUINS. THE SMALLEST PENGUIN IS THE LITTLE PENGUIN!

FUN FACT! They can dive pretty deep - the same depth as the Eiffel Tower is tall!

KING PENGUIN

LOCATION: Several Antarctic and Sub-Antarctic islands
HEIGHT: Up to 95cm
WEIGHT: As much as 17kg

DID YOU KNOW? KING PENGUINS DON'T BUILD NESTS BUT INSTEAD INCUBATE EGGS BY BALANCING THEM ON THEIR FEET TO KEEP THEM OFF THE FREEZING SNOW AND ICE! THEY THEN COVER THEM WITH A LOOSE FOLD OF SKIN.

GENTOO PENGUIN

LOCATION: Antarctic and Sub-Antarctic islands
HEIGHT: Up to 75cm
WEIGHT: As much as 8.5kg

DID YOU KNOW? THEY ARE THE WORLD'S FASTEST UNDERWATER BIRD, REACHING SPEEDS OF UP TO 23 MILES PER HOUR.

FUN FACT! They are the friendliest of all the penguins and hardly ever fall out with each other!

DID YOU KNOW? EMPEROR PENGUINS ARE THE WORLD'S DEEPEST-DIVING BIRDS, REACHING DEPTHS OF APPROXIMATELY 550 METRES.

MAGELLANIC PENGUIN

LOCATION: Falkland Islands and small islands along the coast of South America
HEIGHT: Around 70cm
WEIGHT: Between 4 and 4.7kg

DID YOU KNOW? They are found on the Falkland Islands which is an archipelago located on the polar front, so they're not actually Antarctic!

SOUTHERN ROCKHOPPER PENGUIN

LOCATION: Sub-Antarctic islands
HEIGHT: Up to 48cm
WEIGHT: As much as 4kg

FUN FACT! AS THE NAME SUGGESTS, THE SOUTHERN ROCKHOPPER LOVES TO HOP AND CAN JUMP ALMOST 2M IN JUST ONE LEAP!

DID YOU KNOW? It's thought that their distinctive yellow feathers above their eyes help them blend in with the tall grasses.

FUN FACT! ADELIE PENGUINS CAN LEAP STRAIGHT OUT OF THE WATER AND ONTO LAND!

ADELIE PENGUIN

LOCATION: Coasts of Antarctica before migrating north in the winter
HEIGHT: Up to 73cm
WEIGHT: As much as 6kg

DID YOU KNOW? The name Adelie comes from *Adelie Land* which is an area in Antarctica claimed by the French!

AMAZING ANIMALS OF AUSTRALIA

AUSTRALIA IS HOME TO SOME PRETTY AMAZING WILDLIFE INCLUDING MANY MARSUPIALS - MAMMALS WHO HAVE POUCHES, AND MONOTREMES - MAMMALS WHO LAY EGGS! LET'S TAKE A LOOK DOWN UNDER!

CUDDLY KOALAS!

DID YOU KNOW?
They don't live in social groups and prefer to live alone.

BARELY A BEAR
Koala's scientific name is PHASCOLARCTOS CINEREUS which translates as 'ash-coloured pouch bear', but koalas aren't bears – they're marsupials! They have more in common with kangaroos than bears!

TREE HUGGERS
Koalas spend most of their time high in the treetops of the eucalyptus tree. They even sleep up there, finding a fork in a tree to snuggle into. They can sleep for 18 to 22 hours a day, so it must be comfy!

LETHAL LUNCH!
Koalas get their water intake from eating eucalyptus leaves. These leaves are poisonous to other animals and can be fatal if eaten! However, the koala has special enzymes in its gut which can digest these toxic treats!

FUN FACT!
Koalas have two thumbs and three fingers on each of their feet. The thumbs help them grip on to the tree branches.

MARSUPIALS ARE DEFINED BY HOW THEY CARRY THEIR BABIES. MANY OF THEM CARRY THEIR YOUNG IN A POUCH.

Most mammals are born fully developed, but that isn't the case for marsupials. When they are born, marsupials are underdeveloped and tiny – kangaroos, for example, are born the size of a jellybean.

The baby, known as a joey, will climb up into a pocket of flesh that will keep them safe as they grow. The pouches even have milk for the joey, so they don't have to leave.

Pouches grow as the joey gets bigger and have muscles around the opening which can be pulled like a drawstring bag to keep the baby safe.

MARVELLOUS

There are over 330 species of marsupial in the world with around two-thirds living in Australia!

KOALAS

Koala babies stay in the pouch until they are about 22 weeks old when their eyes start to open. They'll then pop their heads out to have a look around. By 36 weeks, baby koalas don't use the pouch any more.

KANGAROOS
When inside the pouch, of course a joey is going to poop! To clean out the pouch, the mummy kangaroo will stick her whole head in to scrape out the droppings with her tongue! *Ick!* Sometimes she'll have to kick out an older joey to make room so she can get to work.

SUGAR GLIDERS
No marsupials can fly... but some can glide! Sugar gliders can travel up to 45 metres!

MARSUPIALS!

OPOSSUMS
Although they don't live in Australia, opossums deserve a mention when talking about marvellous marsupials as they are the only marsupial found in North America and can have as many as 13 babies! That needs some size of pouch!

WOMBATS
Usually, a marsupial's pouch opens from the top or front of the mother's body. However, wombat pouches actually open towards the mother's rear as this stops it from filling up with soil as they dig their underground burrows.

QUOKKAS
If you're ever lucky enough to meet a quokka with a joey in her pouch, don't scare it! When a mother with a joey in her pouch is feeling threatened, she'll drop the joey from the pouch and make her escape!

KICKIN' KANGAROOS

WHEN IT COMES TO MARSUPIALS, KANGAROOS ARE THE BIGGEST ON EARTH!

DID YOU KNOW?
They cool down by licking their arms! The moisture from their saliva cools down the blood vessels just beneath the skin.

HOP TO IT
Hopping is the most energy-efficient way for kangaroos to get around. A red kangaroo can cover huge distances with one bound - 7.5 metres! They can also jump about 2 metres off the ground and travel at 35 miles per hour!

TAILS TALES!
Kangaroos use their tail almost like another leg. They balance on it to give their hind legs a break when grazing. They also use it to push themselves off again when they need to move. Male kangaroos will often fight each other over females and use their tail to balance on so they can kick their foes with both feet!

PARDON ROO!
Kangaroos' farts and burps are better for the environment! Like cows, all kangaroos mainly eat grasses. However, cows have microbes in their gut which produce lots of methane gas when breaking down the grass they eat. Methane isn't good for the environment. Kangaroos have different microbes in their bodies which produce much less of this gas.

FUN FACT!
Kangaroos are left-handed! Scientists have observed various kangaroos mainly using their left hand for tasks such as grooming and eating. However, they seem to favour their right hand for strength.

MOB RULE
A group of kangaroos is called a mob. They travel and feed in these groups. When they feel threatened, they will pound the ground with their big feet to warn others in the mob.

10 FUN FACTS ABOUT QUOKKAS!

1 THEY'RE KNOWN AS THE WORLD'S HAPPIEST ANIMAL FOR THEIR ADORABLE SMILE.

2 QUOKKAS ARE NATIVE TO ROTTNEST ISLAND, AUSTRALIA, BUT THEY CAN ALSO BE FOUND ON BALD ISLAND AND ON THE MAINLAND.

3 QUOKKAS ARE NATURALLY CURIOUS ANIMALS.

4 THEY ARE HERBIVORES AND EAT NATIVE GRASSES AND THE LEAVES, STEMS AND BARK OF A VARIETY OF PLANTS.

5 THEY STORE FAT IN THEIR TAILS AND USE IT WHEN FOOD IS SCARCE.

6 QUOKKAS ARE MAINLY NOCTURNAL AND SLEEP IN SHADY BUSHES TO STAY OUT OF THE HEAT DURING THE DAY.

7 QUOKKAS ARE PART OF THE KANGAROO AND WALLABY FAMILY, ALSO KNOWN AS THE MACROPODIDAE.

8 THEY CAN CLIMB TREES TO REACH THEIR SOURCES OF FOOD.

9 QUOKKAS ARE AROUND THE SAME SIZE AS A DOMESTIC HOUSE CAT AND WEIGH ANYWHERE FROM 2.5 TO 5KG – MAKING THEM THE SMALLEST TYPE OF WALLABY IN AUSTRALIA.

10 BABY QUOKKAS ARE CALLED JOEYS AND JUST LIKE KANGAROOS, THEIR MOTHERS CARRY THEM IN A FRONT POUCH.

SUGAR GLIDER FACT FILE

These little marsupials are as sweet as their name suggests!

BRILLIANT BODY!
Their bodies are perfectly adapted for life as a sugar glider!

ITS EARS CAN SWIVEL TO HELP DETECT PREDATORS FROM ALL AROUND.

THEY HAVE LARGE EYES WHICH HELP IT TO SEE AT NIGHT.

THEY ARE THE SIZE OF A SQUIRREL WITH A THICK, SOFT FUR COAT.

TAKE FLIGHT!
Sugar gliders don't fly, they glide – hence their name! They have a membrane from their forelegs to their back legs which stretches when the limbs are spread out as they launch themselves into the air.

DID YOU KNOW?
If it's too cold and food is scarce, they can enter a state of torpor. Similar to hibernation, torpor is when an animal lowers their body temperature and rests rather than sleeps.

FUN FACT! SUGAR GLIDERS RARELY SPEND ANY TIME ON THE GROUND!

THE WONDERFUL WOMBAT OF OZ!

YOU'LL BECOME A MEGA-FAN OF THIS MARSUPIAL AFTER READING THESE FACTS!

FAST FOOTED
THEY MAY HAVE SHORT LEGS AND BE A BIT STOCKY, BUT WOMBATS CAN RUN AS FAST AS A HUMAN! THEY CAN REACH SPEEDS OF UP TO 40 MILES PER HOUR!

BATTLE OF THE BOTTOMS!
Wombats live in burrows they dig out with their strong legs. When threatened, they dive down the burrows plugging them with their butts! Their bottoms are very thick-skinned, so can take being scratched and bitten by predators!

FUN FACT!
They poop cubes! Scientists think that it's because they mark their territory with their poo - cubes won't roll anywhere meaning their stinky signal stays in place!

GNAW-SOME GNASHERS!
Wombat teeth never stop growing! This means they have to grind them away munching on the grass, roots and vegetation they eat.

STOMACH OF STEEL!
THEY CAN HOLD ON TO THE FOOD IN THEIR TUMMY FOR UP TO 70 HOURS BEFORE THEY HAVE TO POOP!

DID YOU KNOW?
A GROUP OF WOMBATS IS CALLED A WISDOM!

The name sounds ferocious, but these little marsupials are actually pretty shy!

DARE YOU MEET...
THE TASMANIAN DEVIL?!

DEVIL BY NAME...
Like their name suggests, these little marsupials are from Tasmania – an island off the south coast of Australia. This is the only place they can be found in the wild in the world! They are called devils after their blood-curdling scream!

LEFTOVERS!
Known as the 'bush vacuum cleaner', these little critters will eat anything and scavenge what's left by other animals! Tasmanian devils will eat small rodents, birds, reptiles and insects. They have the strongest bite of any mammal their size in the world, even stronger than a lion or tiger, and can bite through bone!

MASSIVE MOUTH!
When feeling stressed or scared, Tasmanian devils will open their mouths really wide and yawn. This shows off all the sharp teeth they have in their huge mouth!

FUN FACT!
WHEN THEY ARE BORN, TASMANIAN BABIES (OR JOEYS) ARE ONLY THE SIZE OF A GRAIN OF RICE!

DID YOU KNOW?
WHEN THREATENED, A TASMANIAN DEVIL CAN PRODUCE A STENCH AS BAD AS A SKUNK!

AMAZING ANIMALS OF ASIA!

Asia covers about 17.21 million square miles of land and includes 48 countries — so there are a lot of interesting animals living there! The wildlife live in areas ranging from tropical forests and deserts to mountains and grasslands.

GIBBONS

Let's find out about the world's smallest ape!

IN THE SWING OF IT!
Gibbons rarely touch the ground and spend most of their lives high up in the trees. They travel by swinging from one branch to the next using their very long and powerful arms. Gibbons can propel themselves at speeds of 35 miles per hour! They can even swing over gaps of 15 metres! This method of travelling is called brachiation.

MONKEY AROUND!
Despite looking like monkeys, gibbons are actually apes. The main difference is that monkeys have tails, gibbons don't!

SING-A-LONG
Gibbons communicate by singing! They like to sing alone or in groups. Their loud calls help them speak to each other through the dense jungle and their songs can be heard a mile away.

DID YOU KNOW? There are 20 known species of gibbon in Asia!

All about the ASIATIC BEAR

DID YOU KNOW?
Asiatic bears are found in lots of countries in Asia including China, Japan, Iran and India.

TREE-MENDOUS!
Trees provide not only food, but Asiatic bears also rest and sleep up them. They are unique amongst all other bears for their love of life at height!

BEAR NECESSITIES
These bears are omnivores, which means they eat both meat and plant material, but they are mainly veggie and will climb trees to search for fruit. They also love to munch on nuts, seeds and roots.

FUN FACT!
Asiatic bears are also sometimes called moon bears due to the white crescent shape on their chests just below their necks.

DIG IT!
Asiatic bears love to dig! With their powerful front legs and strong claws, they soon make light work of it. They dig through soil to forage for food.

WITH A BLUE FACE, STUBBY NOSE AND GOLDEN-ORANGE FUR, THIS PRIMATE IS ONE OF CHINA'S MOST UNUSUAL CREATURES!

GOLDEN SNUB-NOSED MONKEY

WHO NOSE?!
Nobody really 'nose' why their noses are so flat, but it's thought it helps prevent frostbite as the mountains where they live can reach temperatures as low as -8 degrees Celsius!

FUR FACT!
The fur of the golden snub-nosed monkey changes throughout the year. They moult in summer and then have short, brown-grey fur to blend into the forest. They moult again in autumn when their longer, golden-orange fur is on display to blend in with the leaves turning orange.

VENTRILOQUISTS
GOLDEN SNUB-NOSED MONKEYS ARE VERY VOCAL WITH WHINES, SHRILLS AND CHATTERING. BUT WHAT MAKES THESE MONKEYS UNIQUE IS THAT THEY CAN DO ALL OF THAT WITHOUT OPENING THEIR MOUTHS!

MONKEY MATES!
THEY LIVE IN VERY LARGE SOCIAL GROUPS CALLED TROOPS. THERE CAN BE AS MANY AS 600 IN ONE GROUP!

GOOD NEIGHBOURS!
The closest neighbours of the snub-nosed monkeys that live in the highland forests of China are pandas!

GO BANANAS FOR THESE AMAZING SNOW MONKEYS!

MAGNIFICENT MACAQUES

FACT FILE

NAME: Japanese macaque (also known as snow monkeys).

DIET: Frugivore (mostly fruit) as well as seeds, flowers, tree bark, bird eggs and insects.

LIFESPAN: Between 22 and 27 years.

LOCATION: Japan, especially the Honshu, Kyushu and Shikoku islands.

KYUSHU
SHIKOKU
HONSHU

FANTASTIC FUR

Japanese macaques only have two parts of their body exposed — their faces and their bottoms! The rest of their body is covered in thick fur which gets even thicker as the temperature gets colder.

DID YOU KNOW?

SNOW MONKEY TROOPS LIVING IN HONSHU'S SNOWY MOUNTAINS AND FORESTS BEAT THE FROSTY WINTERS — WHERE TEMPERATURES CAN PLUMMET TO -15°C — BY TAKING A DIP IN THE ISLAND'S NATURAL HOT SPRINGS.

HAVING A BALL
When Japanese macaques get too hot, they simply get out of the natural spring and begin playing in the snow. They've even been known to make snowballs, rolling them around the floor for a bit of fun!

MONKEY BUSINESS
Bathing in hot springs and making snowballs are all learnt behaviours that have been passed through various generations. This is known as cultural transmission.

HOT WATER
The volcanic spring water in the natural hot springs can reach temperatures of up to 43°C, so they'll dip a toe or finger in first before taking the plunge.

FUN FACT!
SNOW MONKEYS HAVE FULLY OPPOSABLE THUMBS, JUST LIKE HUMANS.

ORANGUTANS

FAMOUS FOR THEIR FLAME-BRIGHT FUR, THE ORANGUTAN IS A FIRM RAINFOREST FAVOURITE. THEIR NAME TRANSLATES AS 'PERSON OF THE FOREST' AND IT'S EASY TO SEE WHY...

Orangutans are one of our closest relations — we have 97% of DNA in common! Just like us, they have opposable thumbs (which allow us to grip things) and have been known to escape from zoos by figuring out how to work the locks.

Most orangutan mothers will have just one baby at a time. The baby stays with its mother for the first four to six years of its life, clinging on tightly to her soft, furry body as she swings through the forest, looking for tasty fruit and juicy young leaves to eat.

Orangutans are extremely intelligent and brilliant at using tools! They have been seen using sticks to remove seeds from fruits and even using a leaf like an umbrella to shield them from the rain!

FUN FACT!
They can eat with their feet! Their feet look almost exactly the same as their hands. This makes them excellent climbers!

DID YOU KNOW?
They make a nest to sleep in every night! It takes them about ten minutes, weaving branches together to make a sleeping platform then adding smaller branches on top as a mattress. If it's raining they might even add a roof!

SOME MALE ORANGUTANS DEVELOP LARGE CHEEK PADS CALLED 'FLANGES' WHEN THEY REACH MATURITY. THESE OVERSIZED CHEEKS MIGHT LOOK A BIT SILLY TO US BUT THE FEMALE ORANGUTANS FIND THEM VERY ATTRACTIVE!

The Wild Side Of GIANT PANDAS

Get up close and personal with China's most popular animal.

GIANT PANDA

FACT FILE:

LOCATION: Mountain forests in South Central China
DIET: 99% bamboo, sometimes small animals
SIZE: 1.2–1.5 metres
WEIGHT: 300 lbs

A DAY IN THE LIFE

There's not much to know here as a giant panda spends half of each day munching on bamboo then spends the rest of that day napping! Sounds like a dream!

BORING BAMBOO?

Do pandas ever get bored of their diet of bamboo? It would seem not! Pandas have been around for 2-3 million years and it's worked for them so far! The problem is that bamboo's not very nutritional and they need to keep eating and eating it to get the energy they need. That's why most of the day is spent munching.

DID YOU KNOW?
Unlike other bears, they don't hibernate. This is because their bamboo diet doesn't let them store enough fat, so they have to keep eating throughout the winter.

FUN FACT!
GIANT PANDAS ARE BORN TINY PANDAS – ABOUT THE SIZE OF A PENCIL! THEY'RE THE SMALLEST BABY ANIMAL IN COMPARISON TO THEIR FULL-GROWN SIZE.

PANDAS HAVE VERTICAL SLITS FOR PUPILS – LIKE CATS!

THEIR FUR PATTERN IS FLUFFY AND UNIQUE, BUT HELPS THEM CAMOUFLAGE. THE WHITE FOR SNOWY ENVIRONMENTS, AND THE BLACK FOR SHADY FORESTS.

BECAUSE A PANDA'S DIGESTIVE SYSTEM IS MORE CARNIVOROUS THAN HERBIVOROUS (BETTER FOR EATING MEAT INSTEAD OF PLANTS), IT CAN'T ACTUALLY DIGEST BAMBOO THAT WELL. A LOT OF IT PASSES AS WASTE WHICH MEANS THEY CAN POOP UP TO 100 TIMES A DAY. THAT'S THE SAME AS FOUR WHOLE BOWLING BALLS OF POOP. AND IT'S GREEN.

ALTHOUGH THEY'RE VERY LAZY CREATURES, PANDAS ARE AMAZING CLIMBERS AND SWIMMERS, HELPED OUT BY THEIR HUGE FIVE-FINGERED PAWS! AN EXTENDED WRIST BONE EVEN ACTS AS A THUMB TO HELP THEM HOLD THEIR BAMBOO.

CLOUDED LEOPARDS

THESE COOL CATS ARE FOUND IN THE RAINFORESTS OF ASIA AND IN THE FOOTHILLS OF THE HIMALAYAS, SO THEY REALLY ARE IN THE CLOUDS!

FACT FILE
SIZE: 60-110CM WITH A 60-90CM TAIL
WEIGH: 11-22 KG **LIFESPAN:** 12-15 YEARS

DID YOU KNOW?
This beautiful cat gets its name from its spotted coat which looks like clouds!

BIG OR SMALL CAT?
DESPITE THEIR NAME, CLOUDED LEOPARDS AREN'T A SPECIES OF LEOPARD. IN FACT, THEY'RE CONSIDERED NOT TO BE QUITE A BIG CAT (LIKE LIONS OR TIGERS) BUT ARE TOO BIG FOR A SMALL CAT (LIKE A LYNX OR OCELOT) SO HAVE THEIR OWN CATEGORY – NEOFELIS!

TREE-TIME!

Cats are all pretty good climbers, but clouded leopards are at the top of the tree when it comes to this skill! Once up there, they can hang upside down beneath larger branches thanks to their large paws and very sharp claws! They can then drop down suddenly on unsuspecting prey!

FUN FACT!
Due to the bones in its neck, the clouded leopard cannot roar unlike most wild cats.

DIN-DINS!
Like all wild cats, they are carnivores and like to munch on gibbons, macaques, small deer and wild boar. They tend to stalk their prey before pouncing and can open their mouths really wide to deliver a killer bite!

FLEXIBILITY
THEY HAVE FLEXIBLE ANKLE JOINTS WHICH ALLOWS THEM TO ROTATE THEIR HIND FEET. THIS MEANS THEY ARE THE ONLY CAT, OTHER THAN THE MARGAY, THAT CAN DESCEND A TREE HEAD-FIRST!

TOP TEN TIGER FACTS!

LET'S TAKE A LOOK AT INDIA'S NATIONAL ANIMAL WHICH HAS BEEN ON THIS PLANET FOR 2 MILLION YEARS!

1 People may think that tigers live in Africa alongside lions, but tigers are found in India, China and even Siberia.

2 TIGERS HAVE ONE OF THE BEST SHORT-TERM MEMORIES OF ANY ANIMAL. IN FACT, THEIR SHORT-TERM MEMORY LASTS ALMOST 30 SECONDS LONGER THAN HUMANS!

3 A tiger's stripes are totally individual and unlike any others. Each tiger has a unique pattern of stripes.

4 TIGERS ARE HUGELY IMPORTANT FOR OUR ECOSYSTEM AS THEY EAT HERBIVORES (ANIMALS WHO ONLY EAT PLANTS). IF THEY DIDN'T THEN THERE WOULD BE TOO MANY HERBIVORES EATING PLANTS WHICH COULD DESTROY THE ENVIRONMENT.

10
TIME TO PAWS FOR THOUGHT! TIGERS HAVE LARGE, PADDED PAWS WHICH HELPS THEM SILENTLY STALK THEIR PREY AND HAVE THE STRONGEST PAW SWIPE IN THE WORLD! THEIR CLAWS CAN BE OVER 10CM IN LENGTH.

9
If you do invite a tiger to tea, they usually hunt and eat deer, but they can also eat wild boar, fish, birds, rodents, reptiles and even insects!

8
THEY ARE THE LARGEST OF THE BIG CATS – EVEN BIGGER THAN LIONS! MALE TIGERS CAN GROW AS LONG AS 2.8 METRES, WHICH IS AS LONG AS A SMALL CAR!

5
IF YOU'RE EVER IN THE JUNGLES OF INDIA AND SMELL HOT, BUTTERED POPCORN... RUN! APPARENTLY THIS IS WHAT TIGER WEE SMELLS LIKE!

7
Tigers have a seriously loud roar which can be heard nearly 1.5 miles away, but they cannot purr. Instead, to show they are happy, a tiger will close its eyes.

6
Unlike most members of the cat family, tigers are excellent swimmers. In fact, their paws are partially webbed which helps them move through the water. They love to take a dip to cool off in pools and streams.

WOW! IT REALLY EXISTS!

HORSFIELD'S TARSIER

- **HEAD THAT SWIVELS 180 DEGREES**
- **LONG FINGERS**
- **VELVETY SOFT FUR**
- **STRONG LEGS TO LEAP 4.5 METRES IN THE AIR**

Also known as the western tarsier, this animal has eyes as big as its brain! Native to Borneo in Southeast Asia, it sleeps all day, clinging to a tree before waking up and catching food at night.

It has super-long fingers and powerful back legs to leap between trees in search of insects and small vertebrates like lizards and birds.

ASIA AT ALTITUDE!

Some animals live their whole lives high up in the mountains of Asia and have made special adjustments to survive the cold temperatures and lack of oxygen.

SNOW LEOPARD

The fur of the snow leopard is 5cm thick along the back and more than 10cm thick underneath to protect it from the deep snow.

- The snow leopard is perfectly adapted for cold, high regions.
- Its large paws help it move safely on the snow without sinking in.
- Small ears stop it losing a lot of heat.
- It has a long tail up to 105cm long which it can wrap around itself to keep warm.

HIMALAYAN MARMOT

These resilient little rodents can survive quite happily at heights of up to 5,000m.

- They have dense, woolly fur to keep them from feeling the bitter cold.
- Marmots will hibernate from late autumn to early spring to avoid the freezing winters.
- They live in burrows up to 10m deep with their families. The deeper underground, the warmer it is.

YAK

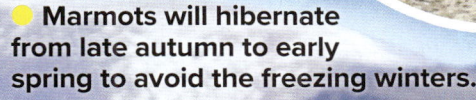

Yaks are a type of cattle found in the Himalayan mountains.

- They have a thick layer of fat to insulate them against the cold.
- They have larger lungs than any other cattle species so they can breathe the thin air found at high altitudes.
- Yaks don't sweat! Animals sweat to cool down so, living in such freezing temperatures, they don't need sweat glands.

Altitude: THE ANIMAL THAT LIVES AT THE HIGHEST ALTITUDE IN THE WORLD IS THE YELLOW-RUMPED LEAF-EARED MOUSE. IT CAN BE FOUND AT HEIGHTS OF 6,700 METRES IN THE HIMALAYAS!

RED PANDA

FIND OUT EVERYTHING THERE IS TO KNOW ABOUT THESE AWESOME MAMMALS!

LOCATION: The mountains of northern Myanmar (Burma) and Nepal, as well as central China, India and Tibet

DIET: Nutritious bamboo leaf tips and tender shoots

SIZE: As much as 62.5cm long, with a tail measuring up to 47.2cm

WEIGHT: Up to 8kg

Found in the temperate forests of the Himalayas and other high mountainous regions, red pandas are some of the world's most skilled climbers. They use the trees to escape predators, seek shelter, and particularly throughout the winter months, sunbathe high in the treetops.

Typically reaching a size that is slightly bigger than domestic cats, red pandas spend much of their days sleeping and eating – sounds pretty great, right? Almost 95% of this mammal's diet is bamboo and, unlike giant pandas, they also eat the plant's tender shoots and nutritious leaf tips. The other 5% is made up of fruits, roots, acorns and eggs.

> THEIR COLOURINGS HELP THEM TO BLEND IN WITH THEIR SURROUNDINGS AS THE BRANCHES ARE OFTEN COVERED IN WHITE LICHENS AND REDDISH-BROWN MOSS.

> RED PANDAS AND GIANT PANDAS AREN'T ACTUALLY RELATED – THEY BELONG TO DIFFERENT FAMILIES WITH GIANT PANDAS BEING PART OF THE BEAR FAMILY (URSIDAE) AND RED PANDAS BEING THE ONLY LIVING MEMBER OF THE AILURIDAE FAMILY.

IT'S BELIEVED THAT A RED PANDA'S 'TEAR' MARKS HAVE EVOLVED AS A WAY TO HELP KEEP THE SUN OUT OF THEIR EYES.

Red pandas have a cone-like structure on the underside of their tongue, which they use to bring liquids to their mouths to check out any scent-marking odours left behind by other animals.

SIMILAR TO GIANT PANDAS, RED PANDAS HAVE A PSEUDO-THUMB — THIS IS A MODIFIED PART OF THEIR WRIST THAT HELPS THEM HOLD ONTO THEIR BAMBOO WHILST FEEDING.

Unlike other mammals, red pandas don't have pads on the bottom of their paws. Instead, the soles of their feet are completely covered with fur for additional insulation and to help them grip onto slippery moss-covered branches.

As well as helping with their balance, red pandas use their bushy tails as a blanket, wrapping it around their bodies when trying to sleep high up in the chilly mountains.

AMAZING ANIMALS OF NORTH AND SOUTH AMERICA

THERE ARE 35 COUNTRIES IN NORTH AND SOUTH AMERICA WITH THOUSANDS OF FLORA AND FAUNA RANGING FROM THE TINIEST INSECT TO THE LARGEST BISON!

BISON BY NUMBERS!

BISON FORAGE FOR FOOD BETWEEN 9 & 11 HOURS A DAY!

MALES GROW TO ABOUT 2 METRES TALL!

THE AMERICAN BISON WAS NAMED THE NATIONAL MAMMAL OF THE UNITED STATES OF AMERICA IN 2016!

MALE BISON CAN WEIGH UP TO 2,000 POUNDS!

THEY MAY BE HUGE, BUT THEY CAN RUN UP TO 35 MILES PER HOUR!

FEMALE BISON GIVE BIRTH TO 1 BISON AT A TIME.

THEY'RE PRETTY AGILE AND CAN JUMP 2 METRES OFF THE GROUND!

IN THE WILD, BISON CAN LIVE UP TO 20 YEARS OLD.

BEAR NE

THERE ARE EIGHT SPECIES OF BEAR IN THE WORLD WITH THREE OF THEM LIVING IN NORTH AND SOUTH AMERICA.

They usually live in forests and have short claws which make them expert tree climbers. If they are feeling threatened, they can climb a tree really quickly!

NORTH AMERICAN BLACK BEAR

- All bears are omnivores (creatures that eat meat and plants) and the North American black bear is no exception, gorging on their favourite berries and insect larvae where possible. They can be found living in dense, forested mountain regions from Canada to Mexico.

BROWN BEAR

- This species, which also includes grizzly bears, can be found mainly in Canada, Alaska and Russia. In Alaska, brown bears are famous for their ability to catch salmon that are spawning upstream as they leap through the air. Clever!

BROWN BEARS ARE SOLITARY ANIMALS BUT DO COMMUNICATE WITH OTHER BEARS BY MARKING TREES WITH THEIR HUGE CLAWS. THEY ALSO USE SCENT BY RUBBING THEIR BACKS ON TREES.

During autumn, brown bears will munch pretty much constantly and can eat up to 90 pounds of food a day. This is to get ready for hibernation when it will have to live off its body fat while it dozes.

...ESSITIES!

DESPITE BEING PRETTY BIG, BROWN BEARS CAN RUN AS FAST AS 30 MILES PER HOUR OVER SHORT DISTANCES.

THE SPECTACLED BEAR IS BRILLIANT AT CLIMBING TREES AND WILL EVEN SLEEP UP THERE! THEY BUILD NESTS HIGH UP IN THE TREETOPS.

SPECTACLED BEAR

● Also commonly referred to as Andean bears, the spectacled bear is the only species of bear found in South America. They get their unique name from the white or pale-yellow markings that sometimes appear around the bear's eyes, making them look like they're wearing spectacles.

THEY ARE ALMOST VEGETARIAN, PREFERRING TO EAT FRUIT, CACTUS AND PALM TREES. THEIR TEETH ARE MORE SUITED TO GRINDING VEGETATION THAN EATING MEAT, BUT THEY WILL EAT INSECTS AND SMALL RODENTS.

The most famous spectacled bear in the world is Paddington! Author, Michael Bond, wanted his character to come from Africa but changed it to Peru after he realised there are no bears in Africa!

ALL ABOUT COYOTES!

IS IT A WOLF? IS IT A DOG? NO, IT'S A COYOTE! LET'S FIND OUT MORE ABOUT THESE CUNNING CREATURES!

DID YOU KNOW?
A dog runs with its tail up, a wolf with its tail straight behind them but coyotes run with their tails down.

FUN FACT!
COYOTES FORM SMALL GROUPS CALLED PACKS.

PREDATOR PALS
COYOTES PREFER TO HUNT ALONE UNLESS THEY'RE HUNTING LARGE PREY LIKE DEER, WHEN THEY HUNT IN PAIRS. THEY HAVE EVEN BEEN KNOWN TO JOIN FORCES WITH OTHER ANIMALS LIKE BADGERS OR WILL FOLLOW CROWS TO FIND FOOD!

HOWL!
Coyotes make lots of different sounds to communicate. They growl, bark or woof if feeling threatened. They howl as a greeting to other coyotes when they all meet up or in response to another group howling.

Their fur has black markings across the eyes that look like a mask. Some think it's to help against the sun's glare – just like sunglasses!

TORONTO IN CANADA HAS THE HIGHEST POPULATION OF WILD RACCOONS IN THE WORLD. THE RESIDENTS THERE CALL THEM 'TRASH PANDAS'!

REMARKABLE RACCOONS!

Don't fur-get these fun facts!

Raccoons are nocturnal animals so they are more active at night.

EVEN THOUGH THEY MEASURE UP TO 70CM, RACCOONS CAN FIT THROUGH GAPS THAT ARE ONLY 10CM WIDE!

RACCOONS ARE FOUND MAINLY IN THE UNITED STATES, CANADA AND MEXICO.

Raccoons have special feet which can rotate 180 degrees to enable them to climb up and down trees head-first!

LET'S LOOK AT THE LYNX

THEIR NAME COMES FROM A GREEK WORD MEANING 'TO SHINE' AND THESE BEAUTIFUL CREATURES CERTAINLY DO!

TUFTY EARS!
The lynx is recognisable by the black tufts of hair they have on the tops of their ears. Scientists think the tufts may act like antennae to help improve their hearing or they may be just to keep their ears warm in the snowy environments they live in, but nobody is sure!

DID YOU KNOW?
THERE ARE FOUR SPECIES OF LYNX LIVING IN NORTH AMERICA, ASIA AND EUROPE. ONE SPECIES IS KNOWN AS A BOBCAT BECAUSE THEY HAVE A SHORT TAIL.

FUN FACT!
THE BOBCAT IS ONLY FOUND IN AMERICA AND IS THE SMALLEST OF THE SPECIES WITH SHORTER LEGS.

HUNTING HEROES
With their amazing eyesight and hearing, lynx make excellent hunters. They hunt at night and will sit and wait for their prey, sometimes for hours, before pouncing, using their long back legs.

CHEEKY CHIPMUNKS!

Chipmunks can be found from the top of **North America** down to **Mexico** in **South America**. Find out more about these rascally rodents!

THE CHEEK!
THEIR CHEEK POUCHES CAN EXPAND TO THREE TIMES THE SIZE OF A CHIPMUNK'S HEAD! THIS IS GREAT TO STORE THE GRASS, NUTS, BERRIES, INSECTS AND ROOTS THEY LIKE TO EAT. THEY CAN EVEN GET AN EGG IN THERE!

DID YOU KNOW?
Even though they love to scamper up trees, chipmunks prefer to make nests in underground burrows!

DID YOU KNOW?
One chipmunk can gather as many as 165 acorns in a day!

BUSHY-TAILED
Chipmunks can measure up to 21.6cm long with their tail accounting for half this length! They use this tail to communicate with other chipmunks by flicking it in certain ways. Chipmunks can lose their whole tail or just a bit to get away from predators. Sadly, it won't grow back but they can survive just fine without one.

CAT FACT FILE

LOCATION:
UNITED STATES, MEXICO, CENTRAL AMERICA AND SOUTH AMERICA

SIZE:
BETWEEN 73 AND 100CM TALL

WEIGHT:
UP TO 34LBS

LIVES:
8 TO 11 YEARS

FUN FACT! FEMALE OCELOTS ARE CALLED QUEENS!

ALL YOU NEED TO KNOW ABOUT THE

PICKY EATERS

THEY WILL HUNT FROGS, IGUANAS, RABBITS, FISH, CRABS, RODENTS, SMALL MONKEYS AND BIRDS. BUT THEY'RE A BIT FUSSY AND WILL REMOVE THE FUR AND FEATHERS OF THEIR PREY FIRST. THEY ALSO HATE WASTE AND WILL HIDE ANYTHING THEY'VE NOT EATEN TO RETURN TO LATER.

OCELOT

These beautiful cats prowl around the rainforests of Mexico.

SPOT ON!
OFTEN NICKNAMED 'PAINTED LEOPARDS' THEIR UNIQUE MARKINGS MAKE THE PERFECT CAMOUFLAGE FOR HUNTING AND AVOIDING PREDATORS. EACH OCELOT HAS UNIQUE MARKINGS, SO NO TWO ARE THE SAME.

MEOW!
Ocelots don't roar like many other varieties of cat but make a noise similar to a chuckle when excited!

DID YOU KNOW?
They can eat with their feet! Their feet look almost exactly the same as their hands. This makes them excellent climbers!

COOL CAPYBARAS!

Check out these 'GUINEA BIGS'!

FUN FACT! THEY ARE VERY SOCIAL ANIMALS AND LIVE IN GROUPS OF UP TO 40, CALLED HERDS.

Just like rabbits and other rodents, their teeth grow all the time. Eating tough plants helps stop them getting too long.

Capybaras will eat their own poop! They do this to get the maximum amount of nutrition from their food. Gross, but kind of makes sense!

They are so chilled out that other animals often sit on them or hitch a ride on their backs!

They can fall asleep in water at the edge of riverbanks! Their nostrils are so high up on their heads, they sit out of the water while the rest of their body is underwater.

THEY CAN RUN AS FAST AS A HORSE! A CAPYBARA CAN REACH SPEEDS OF 22 MILES PER HOUR.

CAPYBARAS ARE SEMI-AQUATIC ANIMALS AND EXCELLENT SWIMMERS. IN FACT, THEY HAVE WEBBED TOES TO HELP THEM POWER THROUGH THE WATER AND CAN STAY SUBMERGED FOR UP TO FIVE MINUTES!

FAST FACTS ABOUT SLOW SLOTHS!

Discover more about sloths!

Sloths are faster in water than they are on land and can hold their breath for 40 minutes!

Sloths are three times stronger than us. They can use just one arm to lift their entire body weight upwards!

THEY ONLY GO TO THE TOILET ONCE A WEEK AS THEY HAVE TO LEAVE THE TREE AND THIS MAKES THEM VULNERABLE TO PREDATORS.

THEY POOP A THIRD OF THEIR BODY WEIGHT IN ONE GO!

THEY SPEND ABOUT 90% OF THEIR TIME HANGING UPSIDE DOWN!

JAGUARS OF THE JUNGLE!

FACT FILE

LOCATION:
SOUTH-WEST USA AND PARTS OF SOUTH AMERICA

SIZE:
UP TO 170CM LONG, WITH A TAIL MEASURING AS MUCH AS 80CM

WEIGHT:
UP TO 120KG

DIET:
OPPORTUNISTIC HUNTERS THAT PREY ON ANYTHING

- Once widespread from the south-west United States, across South America and as far south as the northern parts of Argentina, the jaguar has almost been pushed out of half of their historic range. Many of these big cats call the Amazon Rainforest their home.

FUN FACT!
The jaguar is the largest wild cat in the Americas and the third largest in the world, after the lion and the tiger.

- Jaguars aren't fussy eaters. Eating anything they come across, these opportunistic hunters are known to prey on deer, iguanas, armadillos, birds, monkeys, fish and even caiman (a reptile similar to alligators).

- As well as having similar coats to leopards, some jaguars are melanistic. This means the hair, skin or feathers of any species affected contain an increased amount of black pigmentation. Melanistic jaguars, as well as melanistic leopards, are more commonly known as black panthers.

DID YOU KNOW?
'Jaguar' is derived from the Tupí-Guaraní (an indigenous language) word 'yaguar', meaning 'he who kills with one leap' since they have the ability to kill their prey with a single bite to the back of the skull.

Jaguars, just like domesticated cats, have fully retractable claws, which are protected by a piece of skin when they aren't using them to climb, scratch or catch prey.

You can tell the difference between a jaguar and a leopard by their circular markings, known as rosettes, which have black dots in the middle of them.

With teeth strong enough to bite through hard turtle shells and the tough skin of crocodiles, combined with powerful jaws that help take down prey four times their own weight, it's no wonder that jaguars have the strongest bite of any big cat on the planet.

Their large eyes feature rounded pupils and irises that can have a variety of colours, from golden to reddish yellow. Cubs commonly have bright blue eyes during their infancy.

FUN FACT!
The call of a jaguar is known as a 'saw' because it sounds so similar to the sawing of wood!

DID YOU KNOW?
Unlike many breeds of domestic cat which avoid entering the water at all costs, the jaguar is a superb swimmer and can cross large rivers with confidence.

Surprisingly, jaguars use their tail to go fishing - dipping it into the water, just like a fishing line, to lure in the fish!

THE WORLD'S LOUDEST MONKEY!

If you've ever wondered how the howler monkey got its name, read on!

EAR-BUSTING FACTS!

The howler monkey is the loudest land animal in the world. The only creature louder is the sperm whale who makes clicking sounds louder than a jet engine!

THEIR HOWLS MEASURE BETWEEN 90 AND 140 DECIBELS WHICH CAN BE HEARD OVER 3 MILES AWAY! TO GIVE YOU AN IDEA OF HOW LOUD THAT IS, IF A HUMAN IS EXPOSED TO NOISES OVER 85 DECIBELS FOR TOO LONG, IT CAN DAMAGE HEARING!

Only the male monkeys howl. They have very large throats with a special bone called the hyoid which helps really blast out those calls! They howl to mark their territory, telling other groups of howler monkeys to keep away.

A HOWLER MONKEY IS AS LOUD AS…
- MOTORCYCLE ENGINE
- FIRECRACKERS
- GUNSHOT

FUN FACT! THEY HAVE BRILLIANT NOSES AND CAN SMELL FRUIT OVER A MILE AWAY!

DID YOU KNOW? Howler monkeys mainly eat leaves, flowers, buds and fruits, but they will sometimes raid nests to eat a bird's egg.

IMPORTANT POOP! Because they eat lots of fruit, the seeds pass through their digestive system relatively unharmed, so they scatter the seeds throughout the forests helping to keep them alive every time they poop!

TALL TAIL! Howler monkeys have a prehensile tail which means they can use it like another arm, so it's really useful. They can even hang from a tree branch by their tail, it's that strong! Their tail also has tactile pads on it which means they can feel things as they would with their hands. In some cases, their tails can measure 5 times the length of their bodies!

The Thai name for tapir is **P'som-sett** - which means mixture! And with its confusing looks, the tapir IS quite the mixture! Their long flexible nose might make you think they're related to elephants, but their closest relatives are actually horses, zebras and rhinos!

FUN FACT! A group of tapirs is called a candle!

■ As well as Central and South America, tapirs also live in Asia. You can find four species of tapir alive on Earth today - the Malayan tapir, mountain tapir, Baird's tapir and South American tapir.

ALL ABOUT THE MARGAY

MEET THE CAT THAT THINKS IT'S A MONKEY!

MARGAY FACT FILE

LOCATION: SOUTH USA, MEXICO, AND BOTH CENTRAL AND SOUTH AMERICA

SIZE: 46-79CM, WITH A 31-51CM TAIL

WEIGHT: 2.5-4KG

ARBOREAL: AN ANIMAL THAT LIVES FULLY OR PARTLY IN THE TREES.

WHAT IS A MARGAY?

● The margay is a species of arboreal wild cat that can be found living deep in the forests of Central and South America, parts of Mexico, as well as (in very rare cases) the most southern parts of the United States. They are small, spotted cats that have dark stripes down their back, and are famous for their large, *Puss in Boots*-style eyes.

CUTEST KITTENS AROUND

MARGAYS COMMONLY GIVE BIRTH TO ONE BEAUTIFUL, BLUE-EYED KITTEN A YEAR AND, ON THE RARE OCCASION, THEY MIGHT EVEN HAVE TWINS!

FAR FROM FUSSY EATERS

● Cat owners might already know that felines can be super-fussy when it comes to what they eat. However, when you take a look at the margay's diet, they're the opposite. Primarily carnivorous animals, feasting on mammals, amphibians, reptiles, invertebrates, birds, and their eggs, margays are also known to eat any fruit they find in the forest.

TERRIFIC TAIL

A MARGAY'S TAIL CAN MEASURE UP TO 70% OF THE CAT'S HEAD AND BODY LENGTH, HELPING IT TO BALANCE AS IT CLIMBS THROUGH THE TREES.

SPECIAL SKILLS

● Just like the primates that can be found running and jumping through the treetops with ease, margays are one of the most agile climbers of all the cats on our planet. Their hind feet have the incredible ability of rotating up to 180° inwards, helping them climb down trees... head-first! When this remarkably special skill is combined with their broad feet, large claws, flexible toes and their long tail, there's no stopping this fancy feline from navigating the forest's treetops just like the monkeys they share them with.

ACROBATIC SQUIRREL MONKEYS!

Recognisable by their black and white faces, these agile monkeys live in the rainforests of South America.

NO SWEAT!

Squirrel monkeys can only sweat through their hands and the soles of their feet. Sometimes this isn't enough to keep them cool in the tropical jungles of South America so they have developed a very unusual method to help – they wee on their hands then rub it on the soles of their feet! As the wee evaporates, it helps cool them down!

LITTLE MONKEY

Squirrel monkeys are quite tiny and a fully-grown male grows to about 25cm in length. Their fluffy tails are longer than their bodies and help them to balance in the trees.

CLEVER MONKEY!

Squirrel monkeys are thought to be one of the cleverest monkeys in the world due to the size of their brain compared to their body. They can use tools to forage for food - like using sticks to get insects out of trees. They have excellent memories and can remember their favourite food sources after a long time and revisit them.

DID YOU KNOW?
Squirrel monkeys spend most of their day foraging for food. They need to eat a lot to replace the energy they use.

FUN FACT!
They are sometimes known as death's head monkeys due to the markings on their faces resembling a skull!